ISBN 978-0-282-01058-4
PIBN 10837617

This book is a reproduction of an important historical work. Forgotten Books uses
state-of-the-art technology to digitally reconstruct the work, preserving the original format
whilst repairing imperfections present in the aged copy. In rare cases, an imperfection in
the original, such as a blemish or missing page, may be replicated in our edition. We do,
however, repair the vast majority of imperfections successfully; any imperfections that
remain are intentionally left to preserve the state of such historical works.

1 MONTH OF
FREE
READING

at

www.ForgottenBooks.com

By purchasing this book you are eligible for one month membership to ForgottenBooks.com, giving you unlimited access to our entire collection of over 700,000 titles via our web site and mobile apps.

To claim your free month visit:

www.forgottenbooks.com/free837617

English
Français
Deutsche
Italiano
Español
Português

www.forgottenbooks.com

Mythology Photography **Fiction**
Fishing Christianity **Art** Cooking
Essays Buddhism Freemasonry
Medicine **Biology** Music **Ancient
Egypt** Evolution Carpentry Physics
Dance Geology **Mathematics** Fitness
Shakespeare **Folklore** Yoga Marketing
Confidence Immortality Biographies
Poetry **Psychology** Witchcraft
Electronics Chemistry History **Law**
Accounting **Philosophy** Anthropology
Alchemy Drama Quantum Mechanics
Atheism Sexual Health **Ancient History**
Entrepreneurship Languages Sport
Paleontology Needlework Islam
Metaphysics Investment Archaeology
Parenting Statistics Criminology
Motivational

RECENT JEWISH PROGRESS IN PALESTINE

BY

HENRIETTA SZOLD

[Reprint from the American Jewish Year Book 5676]

PHILADELPHIA
THE JEWISH PUBLICATION SOCIETY OF AMERICA
1915

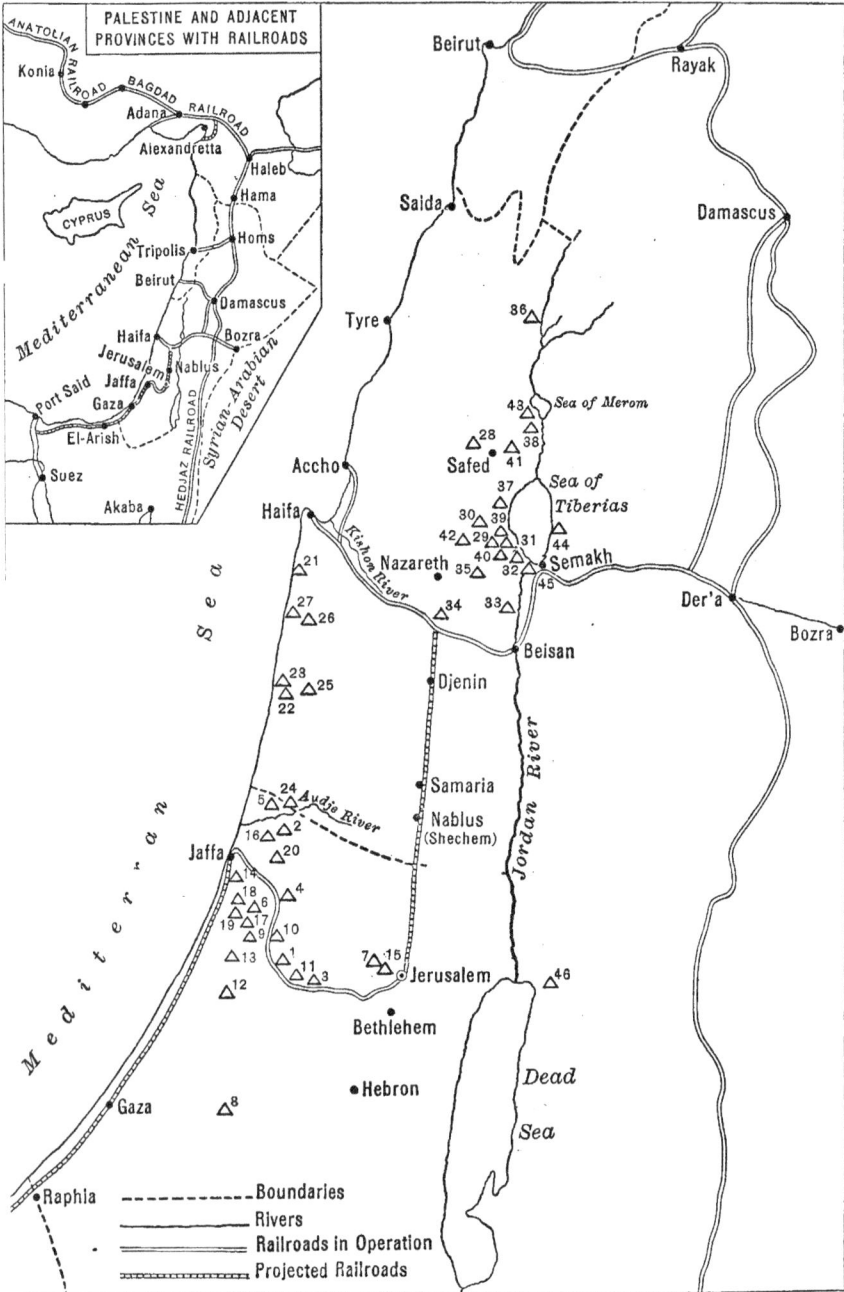

PALESTINE AND ADJACENT
PROVINCES WITH RAILROADS

ANATOLIAN RAILROAD

Konia

Adana

BAGDAD RAILROAD

Alexandretta

Haleb

Hama

CYPRUS

Homs

Tripolis

Beirut

Mediterranean Sea

Damascus

Haifa

Bozra

Jerusalem

Nablus

Port Said

Jaffa

Gaza

El-Arish

Suez

Akaba

HEDJAZ RAILROAD

Syrian-Arabian Desert

Beirut

Rayak

Saïda

Damascus

Tyre

36

43

Sea of Merom

28

38

41

Accho

Safed

37

Sea of
Tiberias

30

39

Haifa

42

29

31

44

Kishon River

Nazareth

40

35

32

Semakh

45

Der'a

21

34

33

Beisan

Bozra

27

26

23

25

22

Djenin

Jordan River

24

Audja River

5

Samaria

16

2

Nablus
(Shechem)

Jaffa

20

14

18

4

6

17

19

9

10

13

1

7

15

11

3

Jerusalem

46

12

Bethlehem

Dead

Gaza

8

Hebron

Sea

Raphia

Boundaries

Rivers

Railroads in Operation

Projected Railroads

RECENT JEWISH PROGRESS IN PALESTINE

BY

HENRIETTA SZOLD

CONTENTS

RECENT JEWISH PROGRESS IN PALESTINE

INTRODUCTION

Educational Development—Agricultural Development—Zionism.

During the long epoch since the destruction of the Second Temple in 70 C. E., Israel has not wearied of avowing, in poem and prayer, his love for the Holy Land. The imagery of his passion he perforce had to borrow from the sacred writers who had been privileged to live in the adored land. But the feeling of the " exile " was none the less real, and as' often as could be he translated it into acts. That edict after edict was issued by whilom masters forbidding Jews to set foot on the beloved soil, was not a deterrent to one who cherished Palestine as the home of eternal verities, and believed that breathing its air made men wise. It seems—the information we have is too fragmentary to permit of an unqualified statement—that there never was a period in which some Jews did not brave danger in order to satisfy the yearning of their soul for the land of the fathers. Now and again propitious circumstances assembled them in fairly compact bodies in Jerusalem, Hebron, and elsewhere. In the fifteenth century we are even told of an agricultural settlement of sixty Jewish families near Gaza. In brief, Jehudah Halevi, the French and English rabbis of the thirteenth century, and Nahmanides, were the exemplars anticipated and imitated by their humbler coreligionists in all the countries and centuries of the exile. After Nahmanides, the attraction exercised by the land of

" spiritual opportunities " became more and more irresistible. Travelers relate that in all parts there could be met groups of Jewish residents, both Sefardim and Ashkenazim, some among them artisans, a few tradesmen, most of them recluse religionists. The expulsion from Spain brought considerable additions, and since then the growth has been steady, though it did not become large until after 1882.

It is only within the past sixty years, however, that the Jewish residents of Palestine have become an organic part of the land. The purpose of the following pages is to trace the lines of their material and spiritual progress during this period.

Three events, occurring at intervals of about twenty years, typify the development of the Palestinian Jewish community during the last two generations approximately.

The first is the opening of a school on modern lines in Jerusalem. At the suggestion of the poet Ludwig August Frankl, Elise von Herz-Lämel, of Vienna, founded it, in 1856, in memory of her father. The object of excommunications on the part of the ultra-pious, it nevertheless was the fore-runner of a still-lengthening series of educational institutions created by lovers of the Holy Land, chiefly through the agency of such organizations as the Alliance Israélite Universelle, the Chovevei Zion, and the Hilfsverein der deutschen Juden. The system includes everything from the Kindergarten to the Gymnasium, and, over and above the primary, secondary, and collegiate schools, an arts and crafts institute, agricultural colleges, industrial and technical classes, a commercial school, two conservatories of music, and courses for Kindergarten teachers, elementary teachers, and Rabbis. These flourish side by side with long-established and recently-established Hedarim,

Talmud Torahs, and Yeshibot. For a complete system of education on the Occidental pattern there is lacking only a University, and towards establishing a University the first steps have already been taken.

The second epochal event is the founding, in 1878, of an agricultural settlement at Petah Tikwah in Judea, by Jews from Jerusalem. The attempt to draw the Jewish city-dwellers to rural homes and occupations proved abortive. It remained for the pogrom years 1881-1882 to provide indomitable pioneers in the persons of refugees from Russia. They founded Rishon le-Zion in the same region, and resumed the settlement of Petah Tikwah, now become the most populous of the forty or more Jewish villages and estates in Palestine. At practically the same time the idea of Palestine colonization was advanced by Roumanian Jews, who established Zichron Jacob in Samaria, and Rosh Pinnah and Yesod ha-Maalah followed quickly in Galilee. These were the first-fruits of the " love of Zion " (Hibbat Zion) movement. In one form the agitation for colonizing Palestine had been begun as early as 1860 by Rabbi Hirsh Kalisher, the same who had induced the Alliance Israélite Universelle, through Charles Netter, to found the Agricultural School Mikweh Israel, in 1870. In the " eighties," when Jews everywhere were aroused by the events in Russia to the need of adopting broad measures of relief, the idea became more articulate. Palestine colonizing societies sprang up in Europe and America: the Bnei Zion of Russia and England, the Kadimah of Vienna, the Ezra of Berlin, the Shové Zion of the United States. In Russia alone there were at least fifteen societies, the most important in Odessa, Bielistock, Warsaw, Vilna,

Pinsk, and Moscow. At the notable Conference at Kattowitz, in 1884, they were consolidated into the Montefiore Federation, and in 1887 into the Chovevei Zion; finally, in 1890, after nine years of feverish activity, the movement was legitimized by the Russian Government, under the name The Committee for the Promotion of Agriculture and Handicrafts among the Jews of Syria and Palestine, with its seat in Odessa, whence it has been called briefly the Odessa Committee.

The third event was the organization of the Zionist movement at the International Congress of Jews called by Theodor Herzl, in Basle, in 1897. The platform of the movement, providing for the creation of "a publicly-recognized and legally-assured home for the Jewish people in Palestine," is the precisest formulation and the most inclusive of the "love of Zion" idea. Five years later the Russian Chovevei Zion societies, or the Odessa Committee, as they were then called, accepted it unreservedly. Zionism aims at making the development of the Holy Land the concern of the whole of the Diaspora. And as in the Dispersion it desires to enlist the united forces of an organized world Jewry, so in Palestine its sphere is Jewish life in the whole. Its impetus does not flow through educational and agricultural channels alone. It consciously seeks to affect and shape trade in Palestine, industry, finance, scientific investigations, general cultural enterprises, in a word, the complete social organization of the Jewish population in the Holy Land to the point at which it becomes economically independent of the Jews "outside of the land," of their alms, and gifts, and tribute, and of their planning and action in its behalf.

THE POPULATION
ELEMENTS AND SIZE

Old and New Settlement—The Exiles from Spain—Sefardic Elements—Ottomanization—Population of Palestine—Languages —Growth of Jewish Population—Recent Immigration—Emigration.

The development here outlined proceeded, at the beginning and for many years after the beginning, on the assumption that the historical Jewish sentiment for the Holy Land was not only a powerful asset, but an actual and sufficient basis for an organized solution of the Jewish problem. Yet there is a difference between the aroma, as it were, of the sentiment as manifested by the New Settlement, the descriptive name assumed by the immigrants since 1882, and that of the Old Settlement, composed of those who come to the Holy Land for purely religious reasons, to devote themselves to study and prayer and to live a life wholly Jewish in practice and thought. They come "back" to the Holy Land, which is Palestine; the new immigrants come to Palestine, which is the Holy Land. The latter likewise aspire to complete Jewish living and thinking, only they wish to express themselves Jewishly not only in study and prayer, but also in work and play. The Old Settlement looks upon itself as the religious "representative" of the secular Jewish world outside. The New Settlement strives to build up a self-sufficient Palestinian Jewish community.

In evaluating the New Palestine, all the elements composing the two Settlements are equally important.

The first large influx of Jews to be reckoned with in modern life came when Sultan Bajazet II opened the doors of Turkey hospitably to the Jews driven from Spain in 1492 and from Portugal a few years later. By the beginning of the sixteenth century communities of Sefardim, with Ashkenazic accessions, were established in Jerusalem, Hebron, Tiberias, and especially Safed, the gathering-place of mystics and scholars. In 1800 the descendants of the exiles, together with the so-called " Arab " Jews, the descendants of Jews that never left the East, are said to have numbered 3000 in the land. Not until the middle of the eighteenth century were they joined by considerable permanent groups of the Ashkenazic division. The newer settlers hailed chiefly from Poland and Southern Russia. They belonged largely to the sect of the Hasidim, and they gravitated for a century towards the Galilean centers, Safed and Tiberias, made famous by Cabalists and saints. Since about the middle of the last century the immigrants from Eastern and Central Europe have been spreading over the whole country, first to the towns and from 1882 on to the rural districts. This brings us up to the date of the New Settlement. During the last generation immigrants in increasing numbers have been coming from Russia, Bulgaria, Austria (Galicia, Bukowina, Transylvania), Hungary, Roumania, Germany, Holland, and the United States. They have swelled the Ashkenazic section until it is said to have reached now 85,000 out of the 100,000 Jews estimated to live in Palestine. But not by any means may the New Settlement claim all the late-comers. Some of them must be counted as belonging to the Old Settlement.

The Sefardic community has not been left unaugmented. The additions from Oriental countries during the last three-quarters of a century are, indeed, not Sefardim in the strict sense of the term, but as they approximate the Spanish-Portuguese in liturgy and ritual, the convenient classification may be applied not only to the North African Maghrebim, from Morocco, Algiers, Tunis, and Tripoli, but also to the

" Arab " Jews; to the Jews from Persia (the Adjami); to the Jews from Bokhara, Mesopotamia, and the Syrian cities Aleppo and Urfa (the latter called the Urfali); to those from Transcaucasian Daghestan and Georgia (the Gurdji or Grusinians); and to the Yemenites from the Arabian Penin- sula. Most of these groups foregather in Jerusalem. With the earlier Sefardim they number there 13,200 it is estimated, though some authorities double this number. If we accept the former estimate, and the estimate of 85,000 Ashkenazic Jews, we are forced to the supposition that only 1800 Sefardim live outside of Jerusalem, in Jaffa, Hebron, Tiberias, and Safed.

The Sefardic section has occupied a distinctive place in the economy of Jewish life in Palestine, by reason of the Ottoman citizenship of its members. Many of the sons of the early Russian and Roumanian colonists have also become Otto- mans, but among the immigrant Jews in the first generation there have been comparatively few willing to exchange the protection of the consuls of their European Governments for the jurisdiction of the Sublime Porte. What will be the attitude towards Turkish naturalization now that the system of Capitulations has been abrogated and the European consuls have no larger rights than in other countries, cannot even be conjectured during the disorder of war times. That a number of Jews refused the liberal terms of the Ottoman Government when Turkey became a belligerent, and preferred to remain Russian, French, and English subjects, though their choice involved the hardship of leaving the country, proves nothing regarding the attitude of those who expect to make Palestine their permanent home. Some of them, for instance, had taken up their domicile in Palestine only in order to give their children the opportunity of an education, denied to them by

Russia, and naturally they were not prepared for the sudden and radical change of plans involved in a change of citizenship.

The picture of the Jewish population requires the frame of the general population. There are the descendants of the Arabs that penetrated into Palestine in the seventh century and mixed with the Syrians, the older inhabitants of the country. Among them are about 105,000 Christians of various churches in the districts with which we are concerned. The Bedouins of the steppes, sparsely scattered through the country, are the pure Arabs, and the Fellaheen, less pure, are the peasant stock. These two divisions are Moslems. Besides, there are Circassians and Kurds, few in number, imported by Sultan Abdul Hamid; a few thousand Druses in Upper Galilee; Turks, mostly belonging to the official class; 2500 Suabian Germans, the Templars who settled in Palestine during the decade from 1870 to 1880, and are living in prosperous colonies near Jerusalem, Jaffa, and Haifa; European Christians, the representatives of the religious establishments founded by the French, the Russians, the Germans, the English, the Americans, the Italians, and the Greeks; and the representatives of Oriental and African Churches, the Armenians, the Copts, and the Abyssinians—and more European and Eastern sects besides.

Corresponding to this assortment of nationalities is the variety of languages spoken. One hears Arabic, Armenian, French, Turkish, German, Greek, Russian, Italian, and English. Arabic is the vernacular of the country; Turkish is used by the official class; French is still the *lingua franca*, and German has advanced to an important place latterly. The Jews, speaking any and all of them when occasion demands, have three more of their own: the Hebrew, rising steadily

year by year to the rank of the Jewish vernacular ; the Yiddish
brought into the country by the East European immigrants,
and understood and spoken now by some Sefardim and Arabs ;
and the Ladino, or Spagniol, testifying, like the Yiddish, to
the tenacious loyalty of the Jew. As the Yiddish is the Middle
High German carried into Poland and mixed with Hebrew and
Slavic elements, so the Ladino is the Castilian of the fifteenth
century, which the Sefardic exiles brought with them from
Spain and developed for daily life by the addition of Hebrew
and Arabic or Turkish elements.

The size and growth of the Jewish population cannot be
left unnoted. Ezra Stiles, on the authority of Rabbi Isaac
Hayyim Karigal, reports the number of Jewish families in the
Holy Land in 1773 to be 1000. Recent figures must be
quoted with as much reserve as Karigal's. " It is said," " it
is estimated," " approximately," must be prefixed to all, to
indicate that they rest almost wholly on conjecture. This by
way of caution in using tables like the following, though so
reputable an authority as Mr. Davis Trietsch · vouches for
the statement that there were in Palestine

10,000	Jews in	1840
25,000	" "	1880
43,000	" "	1890
60,000	" "	1900
95,000	" "	1910

To show once for all how the guesses of the experts differ,
it may be worth while to quote Doctor Ruppin's figures too.
He places the number in 1880 at 35,000, and maintains that
in 1910 it had risen only to 86,000. By a general consensus of
opinion, 100,000 has been adopted as the present (1914) population.

Of his 95,000 Mr. Trietsch assigns 82,150 to twelve towns, as against 202,700 Moslems and 95,000 Christians in the thirty towns of the region we are concerned with, the region in which Jews live. This leaves approximately 13,000 Jews for the rural settlements as against about 290,000 of the general population in the open country in the same region. In 1914 it was assumed that the rural Jewish population approximated 15,000.

These figures may be regarded as coming sufficiently close to the truth to warrant making the general inference that Jewish immigration into Palestine is growing at a fairly rapid pace, a fact that gains in importance when it is remembered that the general population, especially the Arabic portion, has shown a tendency to be stationary. The percentage of increase in thirty years for the general population has been 40; for the Jews, 280. In 1880 the Jews formed 5% of the whole population of about 500,000, and in 1910, 13.5% of the whole population of 700,000.

The two streams of immigrants of present importance flow from the Yemen, in southwestern Arabia, and from Eastern Europe, the latter through the ports of Odessa for Russia, Constanza for Roumania, and Trieste for Galicia. We have approximate figures for the Yemen, and somewhat more definite data regarding Odessa. Both streams began to flow copiously Palestineward in the same year, 1882; both had their source in persecution; and both are largely feeders of the New Settlement.

The early refugees from the Yemen settled in Jerusalem, where there is now a community of about 3000. Since 1908, according to a plan developed and applied by the Workmen's Union of Jaffa (Ha-Poël ha-Zaïr), arriving Yemenites have been directed to the colonies Rishon le-Zion, Rehobot, Petah Tikwah, Hederah, Yemma, and others. It is reckoned that during 1911-1912 there arrived 2000 of them, and during 1913 they came at the rate of 120 a month.

The figures for Odessa are complete only for those persons who applied to the Information Bureau of the Odessa Committee. In the six years 1905 to 1910 there passed through to Palestine 12,965 persons, of whom about 30% were under 30 years of age. A little less than half intended to settle in Jerusalem and Hebron; 4814 in Jaffa, and 1646 in the colonies; 2041 went thither to end their days in the Holy Land; 297 were taken or sent thither for their schooling.

Even these scanty statistics ought in fairness to be offset by figures showing the emigration. But there are not enough data to make even guessing profitable. Only the general statement may be hazarded, that during the last few years, since Turkey has adopted a constitution, which imposes military duty upon all classes of the population alike, emigration has increased considerably, especially among the younger men.

THE RURAL DEVELOPMENT
FIRST PERIOD OF JEWISH COLONIZATION
1882–1899

Jews in Agriculture up to 1882—The First Agriculturists—Baron de Rothschild—Chovevei Zion or Odessa Committee—Other Colonizing Forces—Independent Colonies—Recapitulation 1882–1899—Mishmar ha-Yarden—Hederah—Ekron—Criticism of System Adopted—Rishon le-Zion: Vine Plantations—Administrators.

The New Settlement was wholly rural in character at the beginning. There was little Jewish experience to guide it. In Russia there had been over seventy-five years of farming in Jewish colonies, but they were wholly under Government tutelage. The experiments in the United States were simultaneous with the Palestinian. Argentine and Cyprus came later. Only in Hungary there had long been isolated Jewish farmers on soil of their own.

As for Palestine itself, besides the Gaza settlement in the fifteenth century, Don Joseph Nasi must be recorded and his endeavor, in the middle of the sixteenth century, to introduce mulberry plantations for the benefit of the Jews of Tiberias. In the Arab village of Pekiin there are Sefardic Jews who are engaged in rural pursuits, as their ancestors are said to have been for four hundred years in the same spot. During the nineteenth century three attempts at colonization preceded the Russian-Roumanian movement. Sir Moses Montefiore, after consultation with a few Jewish owners of farms in Palestine, tried, in 1854, to settle a group of thirty-five Safed Jews in Galilee. The Kalisher agitation drew Jerusalem Jews to Moza in 1873 and to Petah Tikwah in 1878. The first attempt ended before it was begun, the other two almost as soon as begun. This is the whole tale of the Jew in agriculture in Palestine up to 1882.

The Russian and Roumanian groups of settlers had as little preparation for their pioneer task as Montefiore's or Kalisher's. They were as a rule not agriculturists. Of conditions in Palestine, its climate, the soil, the land laws, the language, they knew as little as of ploughing and planting and harvesting. Very few had any capital to start with. Many, about ninety of them, were young students, members of the groups called Bilu (from the initials of the four Hebrew words of the phrase in Is. 2: 5: " O house of Jacob, come ye, let us walk ").

If the colonists did not succumb, it was because their enthusiasm went a long way towards neutralizing hardships

and the most grievous disappointments. The Bilus had to
keep the wolf from the door by working as day-laborers for a
pittance at the Mikweh Israel Agricultural School of the Alliance Israélite Universelle. Some of them did not even shrink
from hiring themselves out as farm help to the Arabs in the
neighboring villages.

In spite of the grim determination of the colonists, an
appeal for help had to be sent to Russia before long. Thence
it was carried to Baron Edmond de Rothschild by a delegation
from among the colonists, and he promptly came to the rescue
of Rishon le-Zion with money as well as with agricultural in-
structors. From that moment until this day he has been to the
colonists a very present help, the chief of the " lovers of Zion,"
in devotion to the cause rivaling the organized Chovevei Zion
and the colonists themselves. Not only was he ready to put
means, men, and what he thought expert advice at the disposal
of the Russian and Roumanian refugees in Palestine, for the
undertakings which they started and failed to carry through,
but infected by their zeal he became himself a colonizer.
Ekron in Judea, which he called Mazkeret Bathia in honor
of his mother, and Metullah in remote Upper Galilee were
his own foundations. In the course of the seventeen years
we are now considering he supported not only these his own
colonies, but at one time or another, if not all the time,
Rishon le-Zion and Petah Tikwah in Judea, Hederah and
Zichron Jacob in Samaria, and Rosh Pinnah and Yesod ha-
Maalah in Upper Galilee. Year after year he made land purchases, some to enlarge the area of the colonies under his
protection, while others, on both sides of the Jordan, have
constituted independent domains.

Nothing daunted by Rishon le-Zion's distress, there were willing hands to undertake the resettlement of Petah Tikwah and the founding of Yesod ha-Maalah the very next year, in 1883. Before another twelvemonth had passed, they too turned to Europe for help. At that time the various colonization groups, the Russian and the Roumanian, were to hold their first joint conference at Kattowitz. The Convention at once appropriated a sum for building houses and stables in these two colonies, for buying implements, digging wells, maintaining the colonists until harvest time, and securing the title to their land. Besides it was decided to send five young men to Zichron Jacob to study agriculture under the Rothschild manager there. All this was a severe drain upon the treasury of the young Federation formed at Kattowitz. Nevertheless, and in spite of the hard-luck stories from the pioneers, a resolution was adopted to make land purchases with a view to more extensive colonization. But the vanguard in Palestine apparently did not wait for the encouraging action of the Conference. At the very moment perhaps when it was taken in Europe, a new colony was born in Palestine, the Bilu settlement Katra (Gederah), for which the Federation bought 70,000 vines. In the year following the Kattowitz Conference, $24,000 was expended on Palestine colonization, and $60,000 by the end of 1889. During that period and thereafter, the Odessa Committee, as, it will be remembered, the Federation was called after 1890, stayed and supported Petah Tikwah, Katra, and Wady el-Hanin in Judea; Hederah in Samaria, into which alone it sank another $18,600 in eight experimental years; and Yesod ha-Maalah and Mishmar ha-Yarden in Galilee. And yet, as though not to be outdone by " the well-known philanthropist," it became a colonizer on its own account. In the year 1896, when Baron de Rothschild planted Metullah to the north, it bought from him Kastinieh to the south, on which he had intended to settle Bessarabian farmers. They had failed him. Instead the Odessa Committee brought to it workingmen dismissed from the plantations in Rehobot. The place was renamed Ber Tobiah, and $60,000 was lavished on a venture that has earned fairly satisfying returns, though the colony remains small in numbers and area.

Baron de Rothschild and the Odessa Committee were in time joined by other colonizing forces. The B'nai B'rith lodge of Jerusalem took up lands at Moza, on the Jaffa road close to the city, that had been bought by some of Kalisher's supporters for a few Jerusalem families as far back as 1873. Without wholly abandoning it, they had never wholly developed it. Indeed the tiny colony can even now not be called a developed enterprise, though its experiences have a place of their own in the history of Palestine Jewish colonization. It is no mean distinction either that it offers an excursion ground beloved by the children of Jerusalem.

One of the most important events of the period under consideration was the completion of the Jaffa-Jerusalem Railroad in 1892. In studying the progress of the colonies in Judea it is a circumstance that must constantly be taken into account, though it is not the large factor it will become when the projected extension to Gaza and thence to Port Said is completed. Off the route subsequently taken by this railroad, closer to Jerusalem than to Jaffa, the English Mission had bought Artuf, in 1883, in execution of plans with regard to the Russian and Roumanian refugees. Needless to say, the Mission failed of its purpose. Jews from Bulgaria took the land off the Mission's hands, but they succeeded no better with colonization than their predecessors with conversion. They struggled bravely, and the colony kept its head above water until the helper came. Of recent years sufficient private capital has been invested to enlarge its acreage to the point of productivity.

Little Bene Jehudah, a Transjordanic settlement on the eastern shore of the Sea of Tiberias, established in 1886 by Jews from Safed and Tiberias, has not been so fortunate. Three families only have survived the fierce struggle, and they still raise grain on their 800 acres of land, a Jewish outpost at the edge of Bedouin territory. Help has been granted to them now and again, but never in sufficient measure to be effectual.

There remains only one more colony to be mentioned specifically, the large colony of Rehobot in the Jaffa group. It belongs in a class by itself. Throughout its interesting history, beginning in 1890, it has been self-reliant and independent and successful besides.

Let us picture the disposition of the Jewish colonies in the land in 1899: A cluster of them was suspended as it were from Jaffa in a southern direction—Rishon le-Zion, Wady el-Hanin, Rehobot, Ekron, Katra, and Kastinieh, the last and remotest hardly more than twenty miles away from the port city. Eastward, on the way from Jaffa to Jerusalem, now dotted with Jewish possessions, lay only Artuf, except Moza huddled close to Jerusalem. Northward Petah Tikwah, in Judea, together with the Samarian settlements Kafr Saba, Hederah, Zichron Jacob, and Athlit, linked Jaffa with Haifa. Isolated from all these, separated from them by the Carmel range, was a group of six in Galilee, Yesod ha-Maalah, Mishmar ha-Yarden, Rosh Pinnah, and En-Zeitun near the Waters of Merom, and the two lone outposts, Bene Jehudah eastward on the Sea of Tiberias, and Metullah northward.

Since then Jewish settlement has advanced as far southward as Djemama, twenty-six miles beyond Kastinieh, and negotiations are said to be pending for large domains still further off, in the El-Arish region. But the northern limit of Jewish colonization has not yet been exceeded. That may be due to Metullah's peculiar trials. The neighbors of the settlers, workingmen like those of Kastinieh, were the Druses of the Lebanon district, who disputed Baron de Rothschild's title to the land, though he paid for it twice over. They were not gracious neighbors, to say the least, and besides Metullah was exposed constantly to the incursions of roving Bedouin tribes, more numerous here than in the southern Jewish district. That is not the whole tale of its trials. Again resembling its southern companion colony Kastinieh, Metullah confines itself to a single crop, cereals. It has neither vineyards nor orange plantations. In Palestine it is reckoned that for success with grain each family ought to have from sixty to seventy-five acres. Metullah and Kastinieh both fall short of the average. In the north the attempt was made to adjust the disproportion between population and space by transferring, in 1899, fifteen of Metullah's sixty families to other colonies. The expedient had the disadvantage of weakening an exposed outpost.

The history of the colonies so far as given above awakens two feelings: admiration for the zeal of the Odessa Committee, of Baron de Rothschild, and of the pioneer and martyr colonists; and doubt whether the system pursued was not threatening Palestine with a rural pauperization easily comparable with that caused by the Halukkah in the " holy cities."

The doubt ought not to be allowed to harden into a convietion without a fair consideration of the difficulties in the way of adapting the European settler to an Asiatic environment, and at the same time transforming into a peasant the city-bred Jew, who has been an inbred city-dweller for generations.

The fortunes of the colonists of Mishmar ha-Yarden are an epitome of the conditions encountered by all. Twenty-four men, all penniless, most of them having been workingmen for several years in the earlier colonies, secured a small piece of land on the Jordan, where it issues from the Sea of Merom. They acquired it on credit, and erected a few houses with borrowed money. As a writer puts it, the colony was " a knife without a blade that has no handle," and all that was necessary to insure the conditions for success, another says, was that someone be found to pay for the land and the houses, install the water works, provide the means for building more houses, for buying live stock, seeds, and implements, and for preparing the soil, not to mention the ready cash for the maintenance of the colonists until their farms yielded sufficient produce.

If Mishmar ha-Yarden illustrates the general inadequacy of the means available for the colonization work, Hederah dwells in the mind of the Palestinian Jews as the symbol of misery, sacrifice, and grief. Its story is told by two mute witnesses, the cemetery at the not distant Zichron Jacob and the somber groves of eucalyptus trees that shroud the beautifully situated colony on the Mediterranean dunes with spectral charm under the moonlit and star-studded sky of Syria. The whole territory acquired by the inexperienced colonists was a marsh, due to the choking up of a near-by streamlet with the encroaching sand from the sea. Malaria carried off the larger part of the colonists in a few years. There was no change in the appalling situation until the colony was helped by Baron de Rothschild to plant 400,000 of the rapid-growing eucalyptus trees, Charles Netter's happy importation from Australia, which had already done effective service in drying out the noisome soil of Petah Tikwah, where a similar condition had existed. It is not a little significant of the character of the Jewish contribution to modern Palestine development that in Arabic parlance the eucalyptus is the "Jew's tree."

The story of Ekron has additional points of interest: Baron de Rothschild brought eleven families from Lithuania and seven from Roumania, the first Palestinian colonists equipped with a knowledge of agriculture. It was due partly to their religious fidelity that Ekron nevertheless succeeded no better than the other colonies. In the fifth year of its existence occurred the Shemittah, the Sabbatical year. The observance of the Biblical law of the Seventh Year of Release crippled the farmers in Ekron as well as in other colonies. But that they did not retrieve their fortunes had another reason. The Rothschild "administrator," to use the Palestinian term, changed the crop from grain to fruit. Without investigating conditions thoroughly, he supposed that the former required more area than the colony had had allotted to it. The Russian farmers had however understood the cultivation of grain, and of plantations they knew nothing.

Though the administrator was mistaken in the case of Ekron, it happens that these two points, the crop and insufficient land, were of the utmost importance. They explain why Baron de Rothschild's generosity did not compensate for the colonists' initial poverty. Almost everywhere the mistake was made of adopting a single crop. That caused absolute destitution in the years unfavorable to that crop whatever it might be. Besides, it meant lack of employment for man and beast during a considerable part of the year, and therefore was not economical. And when the only crop was vines, as in practically all the colonies under the Rothschild administration, a bountiful vintage was almost as disastrous as blight and dearth.

Rishon le-Zion was the most notable victim of the questionable policy. Ten men, augmented soon to seventeen, bought 758 acres of land. The cost of installation was excessive, because water had to be brought from a distance, and the soil was not adapted to grain, with which the colonists started out. Baron de Rothschild, it will be recalled, saved the colony. He increased its landed possessions to 1894 acres, and a large part was planted with a million native vines, which, when it appeared that the Arab wines had small value in the market, were grafted with French varieties, sauterne, malaga, and muscatel. Wine-cellars were built, with the most modern appliances and with a capacity of 50,000 hectoliters (1,320,000 gallons). Except that the wine-cellars were of more moderate proportions, the same course was adopted at Zichron Jacob and Rosh Pinnah, and, encouraged by the assurance that the " administration " would buy whatever was produced, Wady el-Hanin, Rehobot, Katra, and Hederah, though not under the Rothschild régime, followed their example. The production turned out enormous, as much as a million and a half gallons a year. In the meantime no measures had been taken to assure sales abroad. The country itself has a small rate of consumption due to the Moslem religious prohibition of wine. Capacious as the cellars were, they were filled literally to overflowing, and the wine had to be sold by the managers for whatever price could be secured. What could be got, would not have sufficed to support the wine-growers, and Baron de Rothschild felt constrained to continue to buy the produce and to pay a living price, no matter what the market rates might be. The price fixed upon was $2.50 a hectoliter (26.4 gallons). Millions were thus poured into the colonies—with the result that private initiative. was paralyzed, and a grave situation created that called for heroic remedies.

It is futile to debate whether this baneful disregard of economic health was due to Baron de Rothschild's devotion to a pet scheme or to his administrators' lack of agronomic experience and business ability. In these respects they seem to have rivaled the colonists themselves. On the whole perhaps the plight of the colonists is attributable to inexperience. As Hederah and Petah Tikwah prove, no one realized the need of guarding against unsanitary surroundings in securing land for a new group; and all the colonies prove that no one troubled to investigate the land laws, which are peculiarly intricate in Turkey. Confusion worse confounded was the consequence, not to mention the bitterness of the colonists, who often thought they had been betrayed in the house of their friends. On grounds not unconvincing the colonists did not consider the Rothschild administrators their well-wishers or the well-wishers of the Jewish movement, which was the breath of their nostrils. The taxes were oppressive to boot, sparing not even fruit-trees, and what they did not consume, was exposed to depredation in a country inadequately policed.

Beyond these, reasons need not be multiplied for the assertion that in 1899 all but the ever-optimistic Jew would have been discouraged by the outlook.

THE RURAL DEVELOPMENT
SECOND PERIOD OF JEWISH COLONIZATION
1900–1914

Ahad Ha-Am's Criticism—Baron de Rothschild and the ICA— Reorganization of Wine Production—Wine-Growers Syndicate —Destruction of Vineyards—Carmel Society—Criticism of ICA Policy—Effect of the Crisis—Cereals and Plantations— Petah Tikwah: Orange Plantations—Pardess—Guaranteed Loans—Anglo-Palestine Bank: Co-operative Associations— National Fund—Long-Term Credits—Education of Farmers: Preparation of Land—Labor Problem—The ICA Educational Work—Sedjera—Other Lower Galilean Colonies—Rehobot: Menuhah we-Nahalah—Arab Labor—Housing Problem— Workingmen's Suburbs—Co-operative Workingmen's Associations—Merhawiah—Land Development Companies—Geulah— Agudat Netaim—Palestine Land Development Company—Ha-Ahuzah—Zion Commonwealth—Settlement and Occupancy— Kewuzot-Kibbush—Reafforestation—Industrial Settlement and Farm School—Mikweh Israel—Agricultural College at Petah Tikwah—Girls' Farm School, Kinneret—Agricultural Training in the Village Schools—Stipends in California—Jewish Agricultural Experiment Station—Land Cultivated by Jews.

These strictures are not the wisdom of hindsight. Criticism along the same lines was heard in all interested circles after the first few years of colonization. As early as 1891, Ahad Ha-Am (Asher Ginzberg), the noted Hebrew writer, one of the leading spirits of the Odessa Committee, went to Palestine to see with his own eyes what there was to be seen. On his return he urged the adoption of two principles: The centralization of all purchases of land as well as of the whole colonization work; and a change from the rather commercialized wine-growing system to the cultivation of grain in connection with cattle-raising and poultry-keeping.

The demand for centralization anticipated a condition that arose that very year, a year of expulsions in Russia. A large number of colonization groups had formed themselves. Each sent its own representative to Palestine to buy land. There ensued unworthy competition, speculation in land, and deplorable manifestations of other sorts. One result was the Turkish Government's prohibition against Russian Jewish immigration and the renewal of the prohibition against selling land to Russian Jews.

Ahad Ha-Am's second journey to Palestine, in 1893, produced two guiding principles for the action of the Odessa Committee: No step to be taken in Palestine without the open approval of the Turkish Government; and no aid to be given to colonists in the shape of money—all assistance to take the form of implements, and even this to be accorded as sparingly as possible.

Finally, his third investigation, in 1899, in which he was aided by a trained agronomist, yielded the advice: Introduce diversified crops; engage adepts to study the land laws; avoid giving assistance to individuals—it blights the will and paralyzes the power of initiative.

It is not necessary to assume that Ahad Ha-Am's findings influenced Baron de Rothschild. He must have been made aware in many other ways of the maladministration of his unmeasured gifts. It is also reasonable to suppose that he was discouraged by fifteen years of what then seemed inconsequential experimenting, though later developments show the early period to have been a profitable time of seed-sowing. At all events, Baron de Rothschild saw fit to transfer all his interests in the Palestine colonies, together, it is said, with a goodly sum for their reconstruction, to the Jewish Colonization Association (ICA), the Baron Maurice de Hirsch Foundation. But this business arrangement has made no change in Baron de Rothschild's personal interest in Palestine. It continues unabated to the present time.

The work of reorganizing the Rothschild colonies was begun forthwith. First of all it was announced that the inflated prices paid for wines would have to be reduced by half at least. The effect on the colonists may be imagined. They had become accustomed to the pleasant security of the unwavering price promised to them whatever the fluctuations of the market might be. In good years the seven wine-growing colonies had produced over a million and a half gallons, for which $172,500 had been paid by the Rothschild " administration." In future the income was to be variable and at best half as large. The paramount task thus became the creation of a real instead of a fictitious market for their chief, in many instances their only, product, and until genuine sales could be negotiated, the most urgent measure was a reduction of the output.

The problem was solved, naturally not without a good deal of painful bloodletting, by the ICA in co-operation with the wine-growers that had been sending their grapes to the cellars. The latter formed a syndicate of 352 members, giving proportional representation to Rishon le-Zion, Rehobot, Zichron Jacob, Katra, Petah Tikwah, and Wady el-Hanin. This company took over the management of the wine-cellars, which it leased for a nominal rent. It was to pay in easy installments for the wine stored in the cellars and reimburse Baron de Rothschild for the outstanding claims. In addition it received as a gift a reserve fund of $320,000, from which current deficits were to be covered for five years.

To reduce the output, many vineyards had to be sacrificed. About thirty per cent of the acreage in vines in all the wine-growing colonies was cleared. The colonists received a bonus for the uprooted plants out of the reserve fund, with the understanding that the cleared area be used for other plantations. In Rishon le-Zion it amounted to $18,400. In this way the production was reduced by nearly three-fifths of the former maximum. As it happens, the phylloxera aided the cutting-down process, though in some places the infected French vines were replaced by American plants. The expenses of the administration of the wine-cellars were rigidly cut down, and the agencies established in Egypt and in European countries were reorganized. In a few years the syndicate, whose official name is Société co-opérative vigneronne des grandes caves de Rischon le-Zion et Zichron Jacob, secured for its members a bona fide price of $1.60 a hectoliter. To this 75 cents per hectoliter was added from the reserve fund to make up for the shortage in the receipts. Now the production was again allowed to rise, and in 1911-1912 it had reached nearly 1,100,000 gallons as compared with 900,000 in 1910, and 650,000 at the time of lowest production. The whole output was disposed of in 1911, over 350,000 gallons being sold in Egypt, 300,000 in the rest of the Orient, and the balance, about 400,000, in Switzerland, France, Russia, Germany, America, and Galicia. In the same year the co-operative society was able to pay to Baron de Rothschild the sum of $90,000 as the first installment of its debt, and in 1912-1913, the vintage handled by the company had a value of at least $200,000. Another indication of a wise business policy is the fact that besides wines and cognacs the growers turned their attention to by-products, like cream of tartar, and in the wake of the more independent attitude has come an opener mind for new industries, such as the cultivation of grapes for table uses, either as fresh grapes or as raisins, for both of which Egypt offers an almost never-failing market.

A large part of the success achieved by the co-operative society must be attributed to the company that acts as its selling agent, the Carmel, with branches in Russia, the United States, Turkey and Egypt, Germany, England, and France.

In a word, the co-operative society is a remarkably vigorous expression of the self-reliant spirit that pervades the recent colonization period in contrast with the former.

It should be mentioned that on the scientific side the radical procedure of the ICA has not received unqualified endorsement. There are experts that hold Baron de Rothschild's untrained instinct to have been the surer guide. Palestine, they maintain, is primarily adapted for vine plantations. If it was a mistaken policy from the economic point of view to concentrate upon them too intensively at the outset, it was a headlong policy to uproot what had been planted. A betterment might have been effected in other ways. Against which the economists hold up the difficulties inherent in the situation over and above those of competition with the wines of other countries. There is first the circumstance that home consumption is bound to be small in a Moslem country. Then there is the problem of transportation from the colonies to the port of Jaffa. This the co-operative society has already tackled. It has put the sum of $21,600 at the disposal of Rehobot for constructing a wagon-road to Rishon le-Zion, and $8000 at the disposal of the latter for a similar road to connect it with the Jaffa-Jerusalem Railroad, together making about 9⅓ miles of highway, the two colonies to undertake to keep their respective roads in repair once they are built. Incidentally it may be said that road-making for wagon travel is a cultural value created in Palestine almost exclusively by the Jew.

The third disadvantage connected with wine-growing is the high tax imposed upon the product, 15% on the wine plus the regular tithe (osher) on the grapes. In one year the co-operative society paid $27,000 in imposts to the Government. The friends of Turkey are confident that she will continue the modernization of her fiscal system already begun, and then the force of this third objection against wine-growing will be lessened.

The ICA's precaution of paying a bonus did not avert either a moral or a material crisis. The change from the philan-thropic to the business basis, coupled with a reversal of the agricultural policy, was a surgical operation bound to leave a scar. A number of the Rothschild protégés could not recon-cile themselves to the new order. Ill-feeling developed, and here and there old bonds had to be ruptured. Only in the course of the years has the temper changed. Few can be found to-day to deny that, whatever may be thought of the incident, the altered outlook has been salutary.

Regulating the wine production was only one half of the ICA's work of reconstruction in the old Rothschild colonies. The denuded lands had to be replanted. The experts sug-gested orange and almond plantations, fruits for which a market existed, and grain cultivation, which carries with it the breeding of cattle and incidentally the production of man-ure. But all the proposals presented difficulties in the execu-tion. Wheat, barley, sesame, and other grains call for soil of a specific kind. Where the colony did not own land adapted

to them, such had to be bought. Cattle needs fodder, and
the colonists had to be taught its production and care. Plants
to be used as fertilizers ought to be cultivated to supplement
the animal manure. That, too, was a new undertaking for
the colonists. As for orange-growing, it cannot be done without irrigation and motor service. Moreover new fruit plantations do not yield at once. An orange-tree bears at the end
of three years, but a full crop only in the seventh. Almond-
trees bring forth copiously in their fifth year, the installation
required is cheaper than with oranges, and the fruit is not so
perishable. For olive-trees the unproductive period ranges
from five to twelve years according to the method of propaga-
tion, but they have compensating advantages: their fruit has
many uses and by-products; while the other plantations must
be renewed at comparatively short intervals, an olive-tree is
known to bear for longer than a century; and it can be planted
in all sorts of soil—when one sees it clinging to rocky preci-
pices, one is inclined to believe that it can grow where there
is no soil at all.

Land, power, and time, all are the equivalents of money,
and the colonists had none. The bonus paid for the extermi-
nated vines supplied it in small part. Where it did not meet
the situation, the ICA was prepared to advance money as a
guaranteed loan, to individual colonists and to groups. In
this way Rishon le-Zion came to be an orange, almond, and
olive, as well as a wine-producing colony. Rosh Pinnah gave
up wine altogether, and devoted itself to almonds, grain, and
cattle. Zichron Jacob, with its daughter settlements, Shefeya,
Bat Shelomoh, Marah, Herbet Mendjié, and Bourdj, raises
grain, vegetables, cattle, wine, almonds, and olives, and at
Nesly near-by the ICA itself has a remarkable orange-grove.

In Ekron there was a complete return to grain, for which the farm and the farmers were best adapted, while Katra on account of its soil stuck to vineyards, and only added almonds in order not to be dependent wholly on one sort of crop. Lately it has planted 714 acres in grain.

The checkered history of Petah Tikwah illustrates important points in the development of the Palestine colonies that are pertinent here. It will be recalled that it was started by some Jews from Jerusalem in 1878. They bought 692 acres of land to the north of Jaffa in an Arab village. Their neighbors proved troublesome and dangerous. Almost at once they were forced to the expedient of buying the whole village, increasing their possessions to 2466 acres. The sale of the parcels of land to others proceeded slowly, and the proximity of the Audje River, with its marshy banks, caused disease, particularly malaria. A remnant of the little group moved to Jehudieh, less than two miles distant. Meantime members of the Russian colonization societies bought land from the original owners in Petah Tikwah proper, only to experience the same dangers and difficulties. They struggled along until 1887, when Baron de Rothschild acquired a large part, nearly half, of the lands of the colony, settled twenty-eight workingmen and their families on his property, and so reinforced the remnant of the Jerusalem and Russian settlers. The cultivation of grain was abandoned largely for grapes in 1891, and about eighty Jewish workingmen from the outside and from among the least prosperous of the colonists were employed in the vineyards. It was made obligatory upon the Rothschild settlers to plant a certain number of eucalyptus trees as a measure against malaria, and the sandy parts of the land were given up to plantations, chiefly oranges, requiring irrigation. The first

2

orange-grove was planted by the Rothschild administration in 1892. Two years later this example was followed by settlers with sufficient capital of their own. The fortunes of the colony were thus decided. It has been developing steadily since then, with only a slight set-back at the time of the wine crisis. On account of the varied crops in Petah Tikwah, the transition from the one stage to the next was attended with less painful readjustments than elsewhere, and in the increasing population the " Rothschild colonists " imparted less of their philanthropic character to the settlement. Petah Tikwah in a word was approximately normal.

The orange plantations flourished and multiplied. The whole garden city is now encircled by them. In 1912 the acreage in oranges was 1198, compared with 1202 in almonds, 250 in wine, 122 in olives, 23 in other fruit trees (apricots, peaches, etc.), and 41 in eucalyptus trees, the whole extent of the colony being 5417 acres. The eucalyptus timber is beginning to be used as building material, for fuel, and especially for props in the plantations, which until recently had to be imported. To some extent the colonists are destroying the trees, because they are no longer needed for sanitary reasons, or because other and more efficacious measures against malaria have been introduced. The colony indulges in experiments, too. There is an ostrich farm, the rose geranium is cultivated for the aromatic oil it contains, attention is given to rubber and bamboo and bananas as possible crops, and the experience gained in planting cotton there and elsewhere is being utilized now by the Tiberias Land and Plantation Company, which in 1910 acquired about 1100 acres at Medjdel on the Sea of Tiberias, largely for the purpose of testing the value of Egypt's product for Palestine.

To return to the orange production of Petah Tikwah: In 1911 its yield was 122,156 boxes of about 150 oranges each, as compared with 168,088 for all Jewish plantations in Palestine. The most recent figures for the whole of Palestine, Arab, Jewish, and German, are 1,553,000 boxes, one-third of which come from Jewish plantations. This should be compared with the 448,000 boxes in 1903. The whole output has been taken hitherto by Liverpool, Trieste, Odessa, Hamburg, and Australia, the thick skin of the seedless Jaffa, or Shamuti, orange making transportation to distant points feasible.

As Rishon le-Zion became the center of the wine-trade, not only by reason of its vineyards, but equally on account of the business organization that regulates production and distribution, so Petah Tikwah owes some of its prosperity to the Pardess, the union of Jewish orange-grove owners, which concerns itself with the exportation of the orange crop. The ICA, owning considerable orange plantations in Petah Tikwah, was one of the founders. In the early days the Jewish orange-growers were wholly dependent on the Arab dealers in Jaffa, who monopolized the foreign trade. The Jewish growers were thus not in a position to shape the trade conditions, the camel transportation to the port, the shipments, and the sales. Through co-operation the Jewish growers established their own sales-agencies abroad, secured control over shipping facilities and wharf privileges, and so lessened the expenses and increased the profits of the growers considerably. Latterly a second such organization, the Union, has been formed. The inspection of the fruit and its packing for the foreign markets have improved under the co-operative system, and a favorable development along these lines may be expected.

A comprehensive idea of Petah Tikwah's standing may be gained from the fact that in 1912, it paid taxes to the State to the amount of $13,002, and taxed itself for its internal affairs in the sum of $16,793.

The activity of the ICA in granting guaranteed loans introduces a subject of fundamental importance. It does not require colonization work in Palestine to prove the need of long-term credits for an agrarian population. It is a commonplace of financial economy. The unique feature in Palestine was the confusion introduced into the whole idea of credit through the Rothschild system, imitated in a measure by the Odessa Committee, of dispensing charity in the guise of perpetual loans. Beneficent as the ICA methods were in their impersonal business character, the real education of the people in monetary relations was begun only in 1903, when the Zionist Organization, through its financial instrument, the Jewish Colonial Trust, Ltd., established, at Jaffa, a subsidiary institution, the Anglo-Palestine Co., Ltd., for all sorts of banking business. In the course of twelve years branches have been opened in Jerusalem, Haifa, Beirut, Safed, Tiberias, and Hebron. It has at present a working capital of $500,000, a sum not large enough to meet the needs of a farming population. Happily expedients have been found to increase the usefulness of the bank in its peculiar Palestinian environment.

Almost at once the Anglo-Palestine Bank began to exert a salutary influence. It distributed leaflets in the colonies treating of the value of self-help in the form of co-operative associations. The propaganda took immediate effect in Petah Tikwah, where, in 1904, two co-operative or mutual loan associations were founded. In 1912 the number of such societies, including those which sprang up in the cities as well as the colonies, had grown to 45, with 1833 members, working with a capital of $21,000 (of which the Odessa Committee contributed $10,000), and having a debt of $186,813 (of which $99,500 is owing to the Anglo-Palestine Company). The loans run from $2 to $600. In addition to mutual loan associations, there are in the colonies co-operative societies for the purchase of fodder. The Anglo-Palestine Company has been endeavoring to stimulate the founding of co-operative stores, in which it has succeeded to some extent, and of co-operative societies for the sale of natural products on the model of the Wine-Growers Association and the Pardess. There also exist co-operative building associations, of which something will be said when the subject of urban development is reached.

At the opening of the bank, only short-term credits lay within its plan. In spite of the peculiar complications inherent in the Turkish law governing mortgages and the ownership and sale of land, it has since adopted a system of well-guaranteed long-term credits, so grave a need in house-building and in developing plantations.

The second financial instrument of the Zionist organization has come to the aid of the bank in its self-help campaign. The Jewish National Fund was founded in 1901, with the purpose —still its primary purpose—of purchasing land in Palestine as the inalienable possession of the Jewish people. Once a foot of land is acquired by the Fund, it cannot be sold—good Jewish doctrine according to Leviticus 25:23: "The land shall not be sold in perpetuity; for the land is Mine." It may only be leased, though as an hereditary leasehold, the rent not to exceed 3% of the value of the land if used for agricultural purposes, and 4% if used for building purposes. This system naturally requires revaluations of the land from time to time. Its advantages are that land speculation is cut off, the intending settler is saved the cost of the land, and can use in immediately productive ways such capital as he may have.

As the Fund is intended to benefit the people at large, so it has flowed from the people, through various channels of self-taxation. The collections of the first year and a half yielded $98,000; those of 1913, ten years later, $200,000. Its assets (June, 1914) amount to about $1,018,000, of which, according to its statutes, one-fourth must constitute a reserve fund.

The purpose of the National Fund, if executed as at first conceived, to the exclusion of all else, would have been nullified by a provision of the Turkish law, whereby land left unworked for three years reverts as a rule to the State. The volume and the character of Jewish immigration to Palestine were not yet such as to secure large possessions against reversion. The National Fund policy therefore had to be modified, from the vantage point of a generation's experience with Jewish colonization. In turn, the modification required by the Ottoman law furthered one of the objects of the Zionist movement, viz., to organize and regulate the emigration of Jews who desire to settle in Palestine. This calls for a program on which a place must be given to all the problems affecting the Jewish settler on the land.

Accordingly, pending the creation of an agrarian bank, it fell easily within the scope of the National Fund to help the solution of the long-term credit question. Out of its various investments in Palestine, amounting to $687,004, it has made a loan deposit of $63,904 with the Anglo-Palestine Bank for house-building credits, and one of $28,227 for agrarian credits. In pursuance of the same policy, it has advanced $53,855 to the Palestine Land Development Company, and $9000 to the Odessa Committee for objects to be described further on.

The credit situation is not an isolated problem in Palestine colonization. As implied above, the occupation of land acquired is imperative. Again, the early colonization period taught as its chief lesson that the Jewish forces coming to Palestine require severe training to fit them for the pioneer work to be done. By way of compensation, the history of Rehobot, which has not yet been told here, proves that the fine spirit of devotion animating the untrained forces need not be left unutilized. If they cannot be prepared to grapple with the difficulties of the situation, then the land can be prepared so as to minimize the difficulties. The education of the human material looks to the creation of a farmer or peasant class; the amelioration of the land, largely to the creation of a rural settler class.

There remains one more problem, and that perhaps the most complex. From the start there had been in rural Palestine a specific and varied Jewish labor problem. The Arab laborer with his low standard of living was far cheaper than the Jewish laborer; he lived near-by, and could be had in season, and incontinently dismissed out of season, a manifest advantage on plantations and on farms with a single crop; and above all his housing presented no perplexities. This explains why of the many thousands of Jewish young men who went to Palestine with high hopes of independence, only about 1500 (with their families 4000) are left. And it explains partly why so large a proportion of the early settlers of Zichron Jacob, Rishon le-Zion, and Petah Tikwah, did not become the genuine peasants needed at the foundation of a normal life. Between cheap Arab labor and philanthropic pampering the sturdiest of them reached only the stage of the gentleman farmer.

To these three questions—credit giving, the education of the farmer, and the labor situation—the ICA, the Odessa Committee, and the Zionist Organization addressed themselves in whole or in part, and various societies were formed to deal with their several specific phases.

First as to the ICA's contribution: During the early colonization period Baron de Rothschild had made large purchases of land in Lower Galilee, which had been leased to Arabs to prevent reversion to the State. The ICA increased these possessions until the tracts in Jewish hands in the Tiberias region amounted to 25,000 acres. In 1898, even before the ICA assumed the management of the Rothschild properties, it established a farm at Sedjera, at the foot of Mount Tabor. An administration building was erected with barracks, stables, and outhouses; Jewish workingmen were employed, and under expert supervision wheat and barley were planted, cattle was bred, and poultry raised, special attention being given to the important and hitherto largely neglected subject of manures and other fertilizers. The Arabs of the adjacent village were called upon to instruct the Jewish laborers, among whom there were a few women.

Two years later the colony of Sedjera was laid out, in parcels of about seventy acres, in closest proximity to the farm of the same name. The land was leased mainly to the workers trained at the farm. The rent was paid in kind, 20% of the gross produce. A lessee who demonstrated his qualifications could in the course of a few years expect to make a definitive agreement with the ICA whereby the capital represented by the farm, bearing interest at 2%, was to be paid off in 51 years. The investments, including the cost of the land, the house and the stable, the implements, the cattle and the horses, and maintenance until the first crops were harvested, varied from $2200 to $3580. In front of each house was a patch of ground for vegetables, from which the colonists supplied their own table and occasionally drew a small revenue. Supplementary receipts also came from tobacco, potatoes, and small olive plantations. The most valuable feature was the stress laid on cattle-raising from the point of view of manure for the fields and of dairy products for use at home and for sale in the town of Tiberias. The colony, like others, suffered through the diseases attacking the cattle. The practical result will be, on the one hand, the organization of a cattle insurance system, and on the other, measures for enforcing a sort of quarantine against the cattle of the Arab neighbors.

During the next two years Mesha, Yemma, and Milhamieh were established in the same way, in the Tiberias region, and in the period 1904 to 1908 followed Bedjen, Kinneret, and Mizpah. In all these little centers the workingmen trained at Sedjera proved better colonizing material than the early settlers, of whom some had been brought to Lower Galilee from older colonies suffering, like Metullah, from scarcity of land. The ICA is prepared, however, to welcome to these colonies settlers from the outside, provided they are equipped with some knowledge of farming, and have a capital of at least $1000. To such it sells parcels of land, improved or unimproved, on easy terms.

In outline this is the ICA's credit and educational system.

The history of Rehobot affords an illuminating introduction to the enterprises of the Odessa Committee and the National Fund that were also designed to meet the situation characterized above. In 1890 various groups of Jews bought a strip of territory to the south of Rishon le-Zion. The largest of the groups consisted of fifty-five persons, members of a Warsaw colonization society, Menuhah we-Nahalah. For a time the land was managed jointly, and only after the plantations of vines and almond-trees had begun to bear, those of the owners who were actually in Palestine took full possession of their allotments. Rehobot suffered from the wine crisis like the rest. But its recovery has been thoroughgoing, and at present it ranks high among the prosperous colonies. In none have there been so many Jewish workingmen employed from first to last. Three hundred were there at the start, and provision was made for them in barracks, where they dwelt and messed together. By 1895 it is said several thousand workingmen had come and gone. The grafting and other such work were finished in the plantations, and the high-priced, intelligent labor of the Jew could be dispensed with. Wages were lowered, the barracks became uninhabitable through neglect, and the mess was abolished. At the same time, foodstuffs had risen in price through conditions not affecting Arab labor. It was impossible for the Jews to stay on. They furnished the colonists for Kastinieh and other places.

The two points to be noted here are the cultivation of the land before the owners took it over definitely, and the relation of the Jewish workingman to the planter on the one side and the Arab laborer on the other.

In the colonies of Rishon le-Zion, Petah Tikwah, Katra, Zichron Jacob, and Rehobot, there are upwards of five thousand Arab laborers. Some of these actually live in the Jewish villages, which largely depend upon the Arab markets for milk, eggs, vegetables, and garden produce. The situation is not healthy on social and economic grounds. Yet it is not reasonable to suppose that the planters are going to seek labor in the dearest instead of the cheapest market.

In the earlier colonization period, the solution resorted to, so far as the Jewish laborers *per se* were concerned, was to settle workingmen's colonies, like Kastinieh and Metullah, though with the fairly certain prospect that new difficulties were bound to result from insufficient land and capital. In the second period it was discerned that a fundamental trouble was the housing question. If Jewish laborers could be provided with dwellings within already established colonies, an approximate equalization would be brought about between the Arab laborer and the Jewish workingman. And if, moreover, his house could be surrounded with a garden plot from the cultivation of which he and especially his wife would eke out the current wage with the sale of market produce, a considerable improvement would be effected.

The providing of dwellings became a burning problem with the advent of the Yemenites. It will be recalled that two thousand of them arrived in Palestine in two years, and were diverted from the cities to the colonies. Industrious and frugal, speaking both Arabic and Hebrew, their wives ready to replace the Arab women in domestic service, the Yemenites were recognized especially by the plantation colonies as valuable accessions, worth making an effort for. And what they needed was houses—they cried constantly, " Battim, battim."

It is natural, then, that the Odessa Committee, the Ezra of Berlin, and the National Fund should have turned their attention to workingmen's dwellings, with the result that various expedients have been adopted. Where the arriving Yemenites were exposed to the inclemency of the weather, and haste was more imperative than permanence, or where unmarried work-ingmen needed accommodations, the National Fund erected barracks. The Ezra, which calls itself a Society for the Support of Jews Pursuing Agriculture in Palestine and Syria, put up small family houses, five in Rehobot and ten in Hederah, to which the National Fund has added five in Rohobot, five in Petah Tikwah, three in Rishon le-Zion, and two in Wady el-Hanin. The barracks for unmarried men on the National Fund farms and in Hederah and Petah Tikwah have bedrooms for three occupants, a kitchen, a dining-room, and a little library. For Yemenites in par-ticular the National Fund built five houses at Yemma, five at Wady el-Hanin, and three in Rehobot, in the last place in addition to the twelve put up by the colony itself for its Yemenite workers. Besides, the National Fund founded two little Yemenite settlements, one of twenty houses, called Nahliel, on the outskirts of Hederah, and one of thirty houses, called Mahaneh Jehudah, near Petah Tikwah. The Yemenites are favorable to settlements of their own; they afford them the opportunity for a community life with their own religious coloring. The houses, no matter by whom built, have more or less of a plot of ground attached to them for vegetable gardening on a small scale. The National Fund has erected in all fifty-eight houses and thirteen barracks, with the moneys of its specific Workingmen's Homes Fund (Arbeiter-heimstättenfond) and of special funds donated to it by indi-viduals.

The Odessa Committee has developed the idea of working-men's homes in another direction. It has established three workingmen's settlements, one accessible from Petah Tikwah, and two accessible, though not easily so, from Rishon le-Zion.

These workingmen's settlements are not to be confused with the workingmen's colonies of the previous period, like Kastinieh and Metullah. They are intended for settlements in which the day-laborers employed in the colony proper may establish an attractive home for less than is possible in the colony itself, in which land prices are high. The houses are surrounded by considerable ground for garden purposes. The terms of payment are easy, and the proximity to the large colony is an advantage in respect to schools and other communal institutions.

The Odessa Committee was, it seems, wholly successful in executing its idea in En-Gannim, about fifteen minutes' walk from Petah Tikwah, where all the settlers are sure of finding employment. It promises to be equally successful with its newest (1913) venture, of a slightly different character, at Nahalat Jehudah near Rishon le-Zion. Provision is there to be made for three sorts of settlers: farmers who desire to support themselves by intensive farming on a plot of less than two acres after the pattern of a California project; workingmen employed in the wine-cellars, who want a house and garden; and Yemenites for whom the National Fund will care in its usual way.

But two similar undertakings, one at Bir Jacob, a little removed from Rishon le-Zion, the other at Kafr Saba, still further removed from Petah Tikwah, the first fathered by the Odessa Committee, the second by the Ezra, are less likely to bring about the intended result. Both are too far from the main colony for the settlers to depend upon it for daily employment, except the twelve in Kafr Saba to whom it has been guaranteed. Besides, the history of the persons in the settlements points to their being incipient planters rather than workingmen in the real sense of the word. The development here approximates the spirit in the earlier period, except that the credit given is a genuine loan, and not a benefaction in the guise of a loan.

The privileges of these " suburban " settlements are offered on the basis of long-term loans at low rates of interest and repayments in small installments, with specially favorable arrangements for the Yemenites, whose houses are constructed on the simplest plan, and as a rule are built on National Fund properties. The improvements can be acquired by them, but not the land on which they stand. In En-Gannim the plot was secured by the Odessa Committee from the Geulah, a land company organized as early as 1902 by Russian Jews.

The movement for workingmen's houses in all forms dates only from 1908. In so far as generalizations may be based on so short a period, it may be asserted that the repayments on the loans are satisfactory, the Yemenites having won an especially good record for promptitude.

This Odessa and Ezra method of establishing workingmen's suburbs is limited in application. It addresses itself only to workingmen with families, specifically such as have some capital, or at all events a reasonable assurance of a steady livelihood, and it does not go beyond the housing question as such. It leaves out of account all the other phases of the workingman's problem in Palestine. The National Fund goes a step further in developing conditions favorable to a sturdy, self-reliant immigration. Having provided barracks for the unmarried recent immigrant, come to seek, if not his fortune, certainly his happiness in the Holy Land, it realizes that, once such immigrants are secured to Palestine, they should see before them the possibility of rising in the economic scale as rural settlers and of establishing a family. With a view to this, the National Fund has recently adopted the expedient of leasing to co-operative workingmen's associations its estates at Merhawiah, Daganiah, and Kinneret in the north, Hulda and Ben Shamen on the Jaffa-Jerusalem road, Kastinieh in the south, and Gan Shemuel, the orange and etrogim grove planted in memory of Rabbi Mohilewer, near Hederah. Latterly the ICA farm at Sedjera has also been given over to such a co-operative association.

The estate of Merhawiah just mentioned cannot be dismissed summarily. It is the scene of an interesting experiment— events may prove it to be one of capital importance. The estate, of eight hundred acres lies in the Valley of Jezreel, famous for its luscious fertility and as the battleground of the hosts of Assyria and Egypt. Soon Merhawiah (Afulé) will be a prominent station on the Haifa-Nablus-Jerusalem Railroad, nearing completion. The National Fund leased 682 acres of this estate to the Erez Israel Colonization Association, a co-operative settlement company, which, in turn, in pursuance of its aim, settled upon it, in 1911, a co-operative workingmen's association of eighteen members. Besides the members of the association, there are seventeen others employed on the estate by the month, who have the privilege of becoming members, and as a rule the number of employees is fifty, in season rising to seventy. Until recently the work, which is grain farming, vegetable gardening, cattle-raising, and dairying, with particular attention to fodder and animal and green manure, was under the supervision of a professional agronomist employed under its regulations by the Erez Israel Colonization Association, the co-operative settlement company that is the credit or loan-giving body. In July, 1914, the executive committee of the Erez Israel Colonization Association transferred the administration of the estate to a commission selected from among the members of the workingmen's co-operative association, the interpretation of which is that the technical education of the farmers had progressed favorably beyond the need of constant tutelage. The commission has the privilege, however, of referring agricultural problems to the inspector of the Jewish National Fund. The plan of the workingmen's co-operative association is Dr. Franz Oppenheimer's, the noted authority on economics. It includes a progressive sharing of the profits between the co-operative settlement company and the co-operative workingmen's association. When the profit reaches 4% of the investment, the estate passes into the hands of the workingmen's co-operative association, the amortization of the Erez Israel Colonization Company's credit begins, and the relation between the National Fund as lessor and the workingmen's co-operative association as lessee becomes direct.

This social, educational, and agricultural experiment is too young to admit of a definitive statement of its prospects. Agriculturally it stands for the European intensive farming needed in a small country, which cannot be expected to bring quick returns. Nevertheless, it has been successful enough to justify a second experiment, at Daganiah, with slight variations. It should only be added that the plan contemplates the introduction of features that will make it applicable to married workmen with families as well as to unmarried workmen, and will provide for a diversified settlement of farmers, truck-farmers, traders, and artisans. The system, it will be noted, educates the farmer without making a pupil of him; the collective capital of the colonization company puts at his disposal advanced technical aids, otherwise unattainable, and thus, it is maintained, large masses of Jews may become the cultivators of Jewish land, not merely its possessors.

But not all intending settlers are prepared to join a cooperative workingmen's association. There are Jews with more or less capital who desire to settle in rural Palestine, provided the conditions do not necessitate the exercise of a too hardy pioneer spirit. To such the Erez Israel Colonization Association is not a helper. In point of fact it is itself in a sense an unenterprising settler. It would welcome the existence of properties at least half-way developed, ready for actual settlement, water provided, wells dug, soil free from stones, approaches laid out, and improvements built suitable for its purposes, like barracks, houses, stables, and outhouses.

Such preparatory work is the function of several organizations: the Geulah (1902), the Agudat Netaim (1905), and the Palestine Land Development Company, the last the manager of the National Fund properties, and therefore an institution of the Zionist movement.

The Geulah started as a land company, merely to buy and sell land. It was soon apparent that only improved land would attract buyers, and its functions were changed into those of a developing company. It has practically confined itself to operations in the neighborhood of the established colonies, except that latterly it has extended them to the cities. En-Gannim, it will be recalled, was founded by the Odessa Committee on a Geulah plot near Petah Tikwah.

The purpose of the Agudat Netaim, a share company like the Geulah and the others to be mentioned, is to lay out and cultivate plantations (oranges and almonds), and then divide up the property into small salable parcels. It owns two plantations, Hefzi-bah and Birket Atta, near Hederah, one at Rehobot, and the Sedjera plantations of the ICA. It also undertakes to lay out and superintend such plantations for others pending their arrival in the country. Even residents of Palestine have employed the services of the Agudat Netaim.

Allied to these, but with still more specific objects, are the Tiberias Plantation Company, mentioned before in connection with experiments with cotton, and the Irrigation Society Palästina (1911), which has constructed a plant on the River Audje for irrigating the orange plantations of Petah Tikwah.

The largest in this class of companies is the Palestine Land Development Company. It buys and develops large tracts of land. Its first business is to give due attention to the legality of the title to the property, and then to manage it and develop it, putting it into condition for all sorts of settlers, even to the point of planting fruit-trees. At the last, when roads have been leveled, water drawn into the estate, and all needful public and private improvements made, the tract is divided up into parcels, to be disposed of in small peasants' and workingmen's holdings, or, if settlers with means present themselves, as larger estates. All this proceeds under the supervision of a professional agriculturist or gardener, who gives the benefit of his advice to the newly-settled owners. When they come to take possession, not only is the land in condition for productive uses, but the relations with the Arab neighbors have been regulated. The Palestine Land Development Company is also equipped to acquire land and estates on commission and prepare them for the actual occupancy of the purchasers from abroad. The Odessa Committee, for instance, recently employed the services of the Palestine Land Development Company for the purchase of a piece of land, Hederah Zeita, near Hederah.

The Zionists of the United States, partly with the Menuhah we-Nahalah plan at Rehobot in mind, are attempting to help on this phase of Palestine development through the Ahuzah movement. It purports to enable Jews in moderate circumstances to unite for the purpose of acquiring land in Palestine for future settlement. The plan is for groups of about fifty to subscribe for a minimum of seven shares a person at $200 a share, payable in weekly or monthly installments in the course of seven years, the whole capital to be paid up in ten years at the outside. The sum of $1400 so invested will secure an estate of sixteen acres, $14\frac{1}{2}$ under cultivation, planted with fruit-trees, and $1\frac{1}{2}$ reserved for house, barn, and garden. For the buildings, furniture, implements, and live stock, the settler is required to have another $1000. As soon as the treasurer holds $500, it is remitted to the Anglo-Palestine Bank at Jaffa, and when a sum has accrued in the bank sufficient to pay for about two acres on each share subscribed for, the Palestine Office is requested to purchase land for the group. The Palestine Office of the Zionist movement is the agent of the National Fund and the Palestine Land Development Company. It discharges the functions of a land and information bureau, in the latter capacity being in close touch with the information bureau maintained by the ICA as well as with that maintained by the Odessa Committee. After concluding the purchase of a satisfactory piece of land, the Palestine Office engages an expert to manage and develop the Ahuzah estate. It is supposed that the payments of the first three years will buy the land needed. In ten years the colony is ready to receive settlers and grant them a livelihood. The calculation is that $14\frac{1}{2}$ acres of fruit-bearing trees will yield an income of $380 annually. If at the end of the period of ten years one or another of the would-be settlers has not saved the thousand dollars needed for buildings, etc., he can either proceed to the colony and depend upon finding employment there, sure that according to the regulations his skill will be resorted to rather than an outsider's; or he can allow the income from his little estate to accrue for three or four years to make up the expenses of settlement.

There are now eleven such groups in six cities of the United States and two in Canada, and the plan has spread to Russia and Germany. Five of the associations have purchased land in Palestine, chiefly in the region between Haifa and the Valley of Jezreel. Some of the members of the first St. Louis and of the Chicago Ahuzah groups have already gone forward to Palestine; the former are settled at Poriah, in Galilee, near the Sea of Tiberias.

Out of the Ahuzah sprang the Zion Commonwealth, an organization of national instead of local scope. Its plan provides for individual holdings of about 2½ acres, which is sufficient for a homestead. This represents a single share certificate. The members who intend to do farming are expected to subscribe for at least ten such certificates. Besides, the Zion Commonwealth has adopted a radical land policy, whereby at least 10% of all the lands purchased will be kept as an inalienable communal estate, to be leased but not sold, on which will be built the city, town, or industrial district of the community. From the communal land all the members will draw rent and profit. The Zion Commonwealth has bought a tract of 400 acres, with the option on 3000 more, in the Valley of Jezreel.

The Ahuzah and Zion Commonwealth plans have not reached even the tentative, experimental stage recently attained by Merhawiah and Daganiah and their co-operative societies.

It should be clearly understood that it remains for the future to demonstrate the practicability of all of them.

The activity of the Erez Israel Colonization Association begun in Merhawiah has been made possible by a special fund of the Jewish National Fund, called Genossenschaftsfond (fund for co-operative societies). Besides financing the sort of colonization that results directly in settlements (Siedlung), it is designed to support the form of colonization that may be called occupancy. The early days at Merhawiah could not be devoted wholly to tilling the soil to which the workingmen's co-operative association had acquired the title. The neighbors were unfriendly, the Bedouins inimical; they had to be conciliated; it required time and courage to secure the conditions for peaceful pursuits. That early period was a record not so much of settlement as of occupancy.

Those who know conditions best in Palestine look upon the Transjordanic region as the most promising for Jewish settlement. The land is cheap, there is much to be had of it, and it is fertile and well-watered. But it can be won and held only by the hardihood and unremitting industry of the pioneer. With Merhawiah and Transjordania in mind, the Genossenschaftsfond has as its second purpose to equip expeditions that are to consist in part of well-trained agriculturists, in part of young men prepared to rough it, and in part of officials, agronomists, physicians, nurses, artisans, etc., who are to be supplied with tools, implements, camp furniture, drugs, surgical appliances, and foodstuffs—all that may be necessary to take actual and peaceable possession, through the plough, of lands sometimes only nominally come into the ownership of Jewish purchasers through money.

No such expedition has yet been equipped, but on a small scale the work has been done on the west side of the Jordan. At this time groups called Kewuzot-Kibbush are doing the preliminary work on several National Fund estates recently acquired, as at Hattin and Bir Adas. Once occupancy is made secure by them, they have the choice of settling, on terms recognizing their pioneer work, as colonizers on the lands they have opened up, or moving on to the next station and in turn bringing it into the circle of civilized communities.

In 1914 it was estimated that from eighteen to twenty thousand tourists had visited Palestine in the spring. It is fair to assume that ninety per cent of them " went up " to Jerusalem on the railroad from Jaffa, and viewed the hill-country of Judea from the car window. From the erroneous impressions of the infertility of Palestine that prevail in many quarters, it is also fair to assume that a large percentage of those who come of their own accord " to spy out the land," bring back a " report " on technical questions without inquiring into the geologic and historical causes that have produced the bare and gray hillsides, awesome as only mountains are elsewhere. They speak without informing themselves about soil and climate and the present status of agriculture in the land. They, and Baedeker too, ignore the whole development of Jewish colonization, the positive outcome of which negatives the casual traveler's haphazard conclusions regarding the possibility of a future Palestine flowing with milk and honey. The time is not far distant when at least the Jewish tourist, holding a Jewish guidebook in his hand, or subject to the tender mercies of a Jewish dragoman, will alight at Lydda and drive to Hulda to view the Herzl Forest of olive-trees and the nurseries planted there by the National Fund since 1909, and convince himself that Jewish endeavor can and will clothe the bare spots that have been denuded through ignorance, neglect, abuse, and lack of means and modern method.

Or he will stop off at Ben Shamen closer to the railroad, and be rewarded not only by witnessing the success of the reafforestation efforts of the National Fund made there too, but also by the sight of the little Bezalel industrial colony of Yemenites. In their ateliers equipped for them by the National Fund he will stand beside the foreman and watch the filigree workers fashion dainty silver articles, and the carpenters wield their tools, and the women weave carpets and sew needle lace. Before he leaves, the same women will hospitably press upon him milk from their own dairies and vegetables from their own garden-plots beside their houses, and insist upon his inspecting their cackling chicken runs. If he still has time between trains, he will test the olive soap turned out in the factory, or he will seek out the members of the co-operative workingmen's association at work in the fields, and listen to their explanation of their social and agricultural undertaking; he will hear about their success in cattle-rearing; and he will inform himself of the methods used with the pupil-workingmen on the farm.

These reafforestation stations, like the ICA and the National Fund farm schools, are sending forth farm and garden workers that constitute the best material hitherto available for the Jewish colonization. But they can be depended upon primarily only to supply the educational need of the adult immigrant. If generations of Jewish farmers are to be trained up, additional measures must be taken. As a matter of fact, facilities do already exist. Indeed, the very first Jewish

agricultural undertaking in the Holy Land was the Mikweh
Israel Agricultural School, established by the Alliance Israélite
Universelle, in 1870, near Jaffa, on the road on which, further
to the south, Rishon le-Zion was located twelve years later.
The handsome buildings and cellars are situated on an estate of
650 acres, skillfully and charmingly laid out with indigenous
and foreign plants and trees. The school has an adequate
annual budget of about $10,000. In spite of its comparatively
long life, its priority in the field, and its plant, equipment, and
funds, the institution has not been an effective factor in the
agricultural development of Palestine. It has stood away from
the swift currents of Jewish life there, somewhat as the administrators of the Rothschild colonies are charged with
having done. The language of instruction and of intercourse
is French, the course of studies lasts four years, and the curriculum is calculated to turn out, not peasants or farmers or
rural settlers of any kind, but only professional agronomists,
who seek positions as inspectors, supervisors, landscape-
gardeners, and teachers at other schools. The result is that
a not inconsiderable part of its graduates have gone into other
callings, and a large majority of those who stuck to their last
left Palestine and exercised their vocation in Egypt, the
Levant countries, France, and the United States. At one time,
under a director friendly to Palestine colonization, pupils of
the school actually became settlers in the colonies, and the
number of pupils in the school rose to 200. The next incum-
bent changed the policy, and the attendance dropped to 75.
Recently a new spirit has again been stirring in the institution,
and there is a prospect that it may co-ordinate itself with the
trend of Palestinian thought, which is considering, not emigration, but immigration, and not the aspirations of the individual

after self-culture so much as the longing of the masses of Jewish immigrants for normal, healthful activity.

At the end of 1912 an agricultural college was opened in Petah Tikwah with a very ambitious four-years' program: Hebrew, French, Arabic, mathematics, history, geography, chemistry, botany, physics, surveying, meteorology, zoology. geology, and mineralogy; soil chemistry, the installing of plantations, cattle-raising, medicine, dairying, plant pathology, administration of farms, agrarian law, commercial law, etc. To practical work only two hours a week are assigned. There would seem to be a repetition here of the mistakes committed at Mikweh Israel. The time has been too short for a demonstration of value or the reverse.

The Verband jüdischer Frauen für Kulturarbeit in Palästina is conducting a unique undertaking at Kinneret, near the Sea of Tiberias, on land belonging to the National Fund. It has established there a farm school for girls, with a two years' course. Candidates must be at least seventeen years old. The pupils enjoy free tuition, board, and lodging, as well as a monthly stipend. The work is predominatingly practical, occupying the pupils from seven to nine hours daily. The subjects on the curriculum are botany, elementary chemistry and physics, cooking and preserving, in the first year; and in the second, the elements of scientific agriculture, fertilizing methods, plant diseases, the principles underlying various crops, poultry-raising, cattle-breeding, and the care of dairy products. The school has for its use sixteen acres of land for ornamental gardening, vegetable gardening, and forestry, and a barnyard. All the work of the farm is done by the pupils, as well as the sewing and cooking required in the household of the institution.

The importance of this farm school cannot be overestimated. For years the critics of Jewish Palestine colonization have justly pointed to the untrained Jewish woman on the farm as one of the radical difficulties. The Yemenite women, even before their houses are built for them, as soon as the place on which they are to be erected is designated, plot and plant their gardens for vegetables, for home use and for sale. That is the spirit of the true farmer's wife, and Russian Jewish girls are acquiring it. As was mentioned before, there were some on the farm at Sedjera. They shouldered their hoes and went forth to the field, and worked all day without asking quarter. The same is said to be true of the girl farmers at Merhawiah, and the vegetable-growers at Medjdel on the land of the Tiberias Plantation Company. It is certain that one of the best farmers in Lower Galilee was a woman, to watch whom was a delight when she stood throwing feed to her barnyard full of geese, chickens, and pigeons; when she tended her well-cared-for cattle in their substantial stalls; when she discussed prices with a would-be buyer, standing over her golden grain, as it lay heaped up in her store-chamber; when she gave her orders to her employees at whose head she went to her fields; and when, in the gloaming, before the door of her own cottage, she discoursed on the value of bananas for Palestine, or told her reminiscences of the early days of the colonization —an embodiment of the Hebrew philosopher's " valiant " woman.

There are several other educational plans, partly under way, partly under discussion, which promise well for the future of agriculture. The schools at Rehobot and Katra include gardening in their curriculum. A Frankfort society conducts a school for girls at Petah Tikwah, in which the pupils are taught cooking and gardening and vegetable-raising. In addition to the regular classrooms, there is a model kitchen, dining-room, laundry, pantry, butler's pantry, and bath, besides a considerable piece of land for the gardening.

The German Boys' Orphan Asylum was removed a short while ago from Jerusalem to En-Gannim, and the change may give the opportunity for agricultural training to another group of young people. The Mädchenheim, the Orphan Asylum instituted for the daughters of the victims of the Kishinev pogrom, is likewise to be removed from Jerusalem to Rehobot, and the intention is to add gardening and other country pursuits to the curriculum.

Finally, through the interest of some American Jews, opportunity has been given to several young men, sons of early colonists, to go to California and complete their studies, begun in Palestine partly on their fathers' land. Their attainments can only benefit Palestine, seeing that California resembles it so closely in climate, geologic formation, and agricultural problems and advantages, while surpassing it in prosperity and technical progress. All those assisted in this way have pledged themselves to return to their fatherland and utilize their skill and knowledge in its behalf.

To a group of American Jews Palestine owes also the Jewish Agricultural Experiment Station, incorporated in 1910 under the laws of the State of New York. The experiment farms are at Athlit, and a subsidiary field, used as a nursery, is at Hederah. The chief work of the Station has been the cross-fertilization of the wild wheat discovered in Palestine by the Managing Director, Mr. Aaron Aaronsohn, an investigation that will require a number of years. The task he has set himself is that of producing a variety of wheat that shall combine, with the wild plant's resistance to disease and to climatic, soil, and meteorologic conditions, the nutritive and other qualities of the degenerate cultivated varieties. Along with this goes an investigation of methods of agriculture, especially of the value of the American dry-farming for semi-arid regions applied to Palestine in point of implements and soil treatment. The Director's researches have already proved so valuable that some of his results have been published by the Department of Agriculture of the United States, and the wild wheat, in which the western States have a special interest, has been observed at several of the American Agricultural Stations with interesting results. Between the Department and the Station at Athlit a system of plant exchanges has been established, probably to the advantage of both Palestine and America.

Besides wheat other products are under observation: sesame, barley, and oats; citrus, with a view to improving the orange production and introducing grape fruit and other species; grapes, not only for wines but also for the table and for raisins; mulberry trees, to determine the kinds best adapted for Palestine silk production; ornamental trees and shrubs for the cottage gardens; opuntia, to secure a spineless variety for fodder; and many others, while practical farmers, gardeners, and scientists have been particularly interested in the study made of plant diseases prevalent in Palestine.

The scope of the Station is unlimited. Small as Palestine is, and though libraries have been written on it, there are still many uncharted regions and unanswered questions. Soil and meteorological conditions are not known with accurate detail. Encroaching almost upon the Station's experimental fields at Athlit are the dunes, creeping up on the fertile Sharon valley where once stood populous cities and wondrous gardens. They need investigation. Fodder and fertilizers are still open sub-jects. Fruit-trees are under debate: some believe apples, pears, cherries, plums, and quinces are not worth while; others insist that they with peaches and apricots have a future second only to wine and oranges and almonds and olives. The variety of leguminous plants has not been exploited especially as forage plants, the possibilities of cotton and tobacco have not been determined, and the pasture lands are waiting for the atten-tion of the expert.

The Kewuzot-Kibbush mentioned above, the "pioneer groups," are a new phenomenon, but the sentiment under-lying their organization prevails throughout Palestine: "We must win the land we desire to live on not with money alone, but also with the plough."

To what extent has land been so won?

Before this question can be answered, we must know on what land it is that Jewish immigrants are setting out to win an abode for themselves. What is meant by the term Palestine?

The question has had many answers given to it. As a matter of fact, the term Palestine does not, in modern Turkey, correspond to a definite political division of the land, just as it was a term for a variable concept in the days of Israel's independence. Some make it include El-Arish on the Egyptian frontier; some extend it northward to Beirut; some give it an area of 10,425 square miles; some of 14,054; some of 16,217. If we accept the most generous dimensions, it can be placed in California nine times with 12,344 square miles to spare. In general, it is agreed that it is the southern part of Syria lying to the west of the Jordan, together with lands in Transjordania. In realization of the indefiniteness of the concept, most of the Jewish colonization societies, it will be recalled, describe their sphere loosely as Palestine and Syria.

Of this area Jewish hands are cultivating about 175 to 200 square miles, and the work is being done by more than 10,000 Jewish colonists, in a land that has 67 persons to a square mile. The northernmost possession, Metullah, lies in a line with the old Tyre; the southernmost, Djemama, in a line with Gaza, also the old, but recently renewing its ancient fame as a center of barley-planting and a port for shipments. The road from Jaffa to Jerusalem is dotted with Jewish settlements. Two centers are thickly sown, Judea near Jaffa and Galilee near the Sea of Tiberias. In the Plain of Sharon, between Jaffa and Haifa, there are ten Jewish possessions, the Valley of Jezreel has been entered, and the pioneer has pushed across the Jordan. The Jew thus is planted with both his feet on the soil of his fathers.

THE RURAL DEVELOPMENT
LIFE IN THE JEWISH VILLAGES

Jewish Villages—A Small Village—A Large Village—Charitable Societies—Village Budgets—Village Schools—The City Council—The Mukhtar—A Specimen Budget—Education and the Jewish Farmer—Recreations—Hagigah—Union of Judean Colonies—The Night-Watch—Relation to Arabs—Proselytes—Yemenites—The Sabbath.

So far only the economic shell of Jewish colonization in Palestine has been described. The content is life, complete, vivid, and Jewish.

We have been speaking of colonies, a term repudiated by the Palestinian Jews. It has a tentative sound in their ears, while what they have, or what possesses them, is a home-feeling, physical and spiritual. They insist that they live in

Jewish villages, and they are proud with a peculiar pride of their clusters of red-roofed houses gleaming like beacons in the Palestinian atmosphere from an amazing distance. Enshrined in those homes is something new in the way of Jewishness, of which they are the originators. Their pride is the pride of the creator, not the upstart pride of ownership. .

The home-feeling is strongly marked even when the settlement boasts only a single short street, as in the young Lower Galilean villages. On each side the simple little houses are set close together for social, mutually helpful action. The plots in front, forming parallel garden lines, face each other along the whole length. Beyond, all around, lie the deep-furrowed Jewish fields. Such is the village of Sedjera nestled at the rim of the overturned bowl of Mount Tabor. Sometimes the pattern, primitive as it is, was executed wretchedly, as at Athlit in the Plain of Sharon on the southernmost spur of the Carmel. The backs of the single row of two-roomed cottages rose almost even with the precipice, forbidding expansion of family and possessions. Instead of gardens the stables were ranged opposite to the bleak, porchless front doors. At the base of the crag, a little way across the dunes, the whole of an Arab village population is housed, owl-like, in the crevices of the ruins of Athlit, the crusaders' fortress jutting out into the sea. Jewish Athlit is an improvement on such a tenement, say its builders in lame self-defense. In general, it is true that the Arab village even at its best serves as an excellent foil to the Jewish village. The windowless Arab houses like cliff-swallows' nests are built against the earthen quarry from which they are hewn—gray on gray. The tribal enemy approaching with hostile intent fails to see them long after he has been espied and preparations have been made for his warm reception. In contrast to this, the Jewish village is frank and wholesome, planned for the uses of life, not merely to ward off death.

The single street of the primitive Jewish village quickly sends out branches, especially in the less exposed south country, in Judea. The suburban type develops, of which the old Rothschild colonies are the completest exemplars, set in their wreath of glistening orange-groves or more delicately branched almond plantations. In Rishon le-Zion and Petah Tikwah some of the houses are villa-like, and the smaller cottages are trim and attractive with their garden inclosures. The streets are lined with trees, and feathery acacias and mimosas border the lanes to the vineyards.

These grown-up villages have their sights. There is the synagogue, placed sometimes, as in Rehobot, on the highest point, dominating the village physically and its life spiritually, as the Catholic church dominates the South German village, and the meeting-house the New England village. There are the schools with their ample, shaded yards. There is sometimes, as at Zichron Jacob and elsewhere, a hospital, and sometimes a bath, and a community-house for recreation, and a meeting-house for the town assemblies. In Rishon le-Zion there is a palm garden, a charming token of the golden Rothschild days. From the same lavish period dates the beautifully planted public park in Zichron Jacob. There are the water works, the cherished fountains of health for the residents and the guarantors of growth for the plantations. Occasionally there is also the Arab market, Orientally picturesque, and along with it goes what one must call a " slum " district. By way of compensation one pays a visit to the spruce working-men's suburb at En-Gannim, near Petah Tikwah. The liberal credit-system adopted there, coupled with the energetic initiative of the builder-owners, has produced pleasing variety and individuality. The wide street no sooner laid out was planted with young trees, and the front gardens could at once be watered from the works visible at its head. They are the chief boast of the little settlement, which was largely fashioned by the residents themselves in their leisure hours. Now they are privileged to spend them on ample "suburbanite" verandahs.

And these grown-up villages as well as the smaller ones have their charities, too—a Sick-Visiting Society (Bikkur Holim, or Mishmeret Holim), a Shelter for the Stranger (Haknasat Orhim), and a mutual loan society (Gemillat Hasadim), which has latterly been replaced in part by the co-operative societies described before.

Mention has been made of Petah Tikwah's budget of $16,793 for internal affairs. Petah Tikwah is the most populous of the Jewish villages; it has 2670 inhabitants. No other has attained to equally complex and costly needs. But there is none so small as to have no communal institutions. They all tax themselves for public purposes—for schools, medical service, water, roads, and recreation.

The school is the foremost and the inevitable communal enterprise. There are sure to be a few elementary classes in the smallest settlement. In the larger villages a Kindergarten is added at one end and higher classes at the other, until they number the full quota of eight, and there is a Talmud Torah besides, sometimes more than one. Many of the schools are rudimentary institutions, with teachers whose youthful idealism has subdued personal desire, but, unaided by professional training, has not always achieved the refinements of modern

3

pedagogy. Nevertheless, on the whole, the teaching corps is adequate to its task. In the more developed centers the little school buildings are not unattractive, and their equipment, even in so ultra-modern a respect as the laboratory for young children, is admirable. To be sure, where the educational plant is so complete, the village has usually enlisted the help of the ICA, or the Ezra, or the Hilfsverein, or the Odessa Committee. The same agencies, especially the ICA, aid the smaller settlements to maintain a physician and a drug room with a druggist in attendance at certain hours, and at Petah Tikwah the ICA presented to the community its large orange-grove as a public domain, the profits to be applied to the general needs.

These communal undertakings naturally demand regulating, administrative activity. All the full-fledged villages have a Waad, a committee, elected by what is almost equivalent to a town meeting. At first only the propertied residents, men and women, had the vote. In recent years the workingmen, lacking the property qualification, have yet secured the suffrage right, the only condition being two years' residence in the village. But though they may thus determine the make-up of the Waad, they are not themselves eligible to it.

The Waad is at once a legislative and executive body. Its functions include the assessment and registration of property, budget-making, and the collection of taxes. In the thirty years' history of Jewish colonization in Palestine there has been practically no opposition to the resolutions of the Waad; only once was an appeal from a Jewish town council's decision carried outside to the political authorities, and they refused to entertain it. Differences between individuals are composed by Jewish courts of arbitration, and it has happened frequently enough that Arabs have laid their difficulties before the Waad for adjustment. These Jewish village courts have dealt only with civil cases. Indeed, in the whole history of the new Jewish Palestine there has been but a single case of Jewish criminality !

When the interests of the colonies expand, the Waad ceases to act as a single undivided body on all concerns. It appoints committees for the better exercise of some of its functions: a committee on education, one on the administration of justice, one on the constitution, one on the relation to the Wine-Growers Association, one on the co-operative purchase of fodder for the cattle of the colony, etc.

The connection between the village and the Government is established, as in the Arab village, through a mukhtar, often a member of the Waad. This is not peculiar to the villages. In Turkey a certain degree of autonomy is granted to ethnographic, national, and religious groups. Hence the severance of nationalities and religious communities from each other in their peculiar "quarters" in the cities is more marked than in most countries, and hence we have the internal government of the Jewish rural and city communities. The mukhtar is primarily the fiscal agent, through whom the taxes for which a given community is liable are transmitted. Turkish taxes are imposed on all Ottoman subjects alike, but the mukhtar institution affords a community the chance of exempting its own poor, and collecting from its more prosperous members the sum total, to be turned over to the Government through its accredited agent.

Mr. Curt Nawratzki, in his remarkable book on Jewish colonization in Palestine, quotes a specimen budget, that of Kastinieh, which is full of human interest. Kastinieh, or Ber

Tobiah, as it is often called, is, it will be remembered, the southernmost of the Judean colonies, closer to Gaza than to Jaffa. It raises only wheat, sesame, barley, peas, beans, etc.; there are no fruit plantations. It has a population of 150, and owns 1278 acres of land. All the colonists work the land themselves, and most of them constantly employ at least one "hired man," who is paid in kind to the value of about $80 a year. In 1910 two colonists made between $620 and $640; one made $740; three between $860 and $880; two between $1000 and $1040; and two brothers in partnership, $1320. The gross income of the whole settlement was $11,000. The Government tax amounted to one-eighth of the threshed produce; and there were expenditures on account of negotiations with the tax-farmer, etc. The military tax had by that time been abrogated in Turkey, but in Kastinieh the Waad continued to impose it to make up a fund for the support of the families whose breadwinners were serving in the army, or would serve, on behalf of the colony.

The budget for the internal needs of the community was as follows:

Pump and water supply	$965.76
Bath	51.15
Teacher	288.00
Physician (Leech)	180.27
Butcher (Shohet)	108.00
Mukhtar	**48.00**
Secretary	33.05
Dues to Union of Judean Colonies	23.79
For drawing map of colony	15.17
Post	10.16
Night-watch	268.48
Military tax	161.98
Entertainment of officials	27.74
Expenses incident to conflict between two colonists	84.05
Unspecified expenses	364.60
	$2630.20

The only help given to Kastinieh comes from the Odessa Committee, which pays $624 for the third, fourth, fifth, and sixth items in the list, thus leaving $2000 for the farmers themselves, about $100 a family.

Here is betrayed a serious disadvantage inherent in the small settlement. The burden imposed by intellectual aspirations is too heavy to be borne by a restricted community. But if peasant is doomed to remain the synonym of hind and rustic boor, the Jew will never become a genuine peasant, even in Palestine. He must be in a position to give his children a thorough schooling; the practical application of scientific research and technical ingenuity must not be beyond his reach. He must not be expected to cut himself off from the world of thought and creation. These as a modern man he claims as his heritage, and when he insists upon their compatibility with a peasant's occupation, he is in line with the most enlightened endeavors of the economist and statesman of our day. How then, in the early stage of Jewish colonization, can his problem be solved, if he is to be spared oppressive taxation? The ICA met it in one way in Yemma and Bedjen. They are placed within a bowshot of each other. One set of communal institutions serves both, and the cost of maintenance is distributed among a larger number of taxpayers than in an isolated colony. The advantage, it is true, must be paid for in time instead of money: the fields lie to one side of the colony, not around it, and so some of them are at a greater distance from the farmers' houses than they would be otherwise. The co-operative enterprises described in the previous section will also carry the Jew a long way towards peasantry without exacting too large a spiritual sacrifice. However, the future may be trusted to solve the problem radically, for the reason that the Jew himself may be trusted to lead a life in which intellectual training and pursuits have an unalterable place.

After the school and the physician, the drug room, the bath, and the hospital are provided for, attention and funds are appropriated for the recreation center, the Bet ha-Am, a modest " People's Palace." There is one in each of the larger villages. It is the meeting-place of the societies, the literary, the athletic, and the musical. It has a library and a newspaper room, and occasionally concerts and lectures are given in it. As was mentioned before, even the barracks put up by the National Fund for unmarried workingmen are provided with libraries. As for music, the Jew has made Palestine vocal. There is singing everywhere, in garden and field and the school-yard throughout the day, and in the evening the strains of amateur orchestras are sure to issue from one or another open window.

The life in the Jewish villages thus has its gracious aspects. The Jew outside—even, or especially, one who believes Jewish colonization in Palestine to be the means of securing another happy home for his people, in which besides normal tears also normal laughter may be his portion—is apt to think of the undertaking as a desiccated " experiment " or an abstract " problem." He ought to be present at the Hagigah during Hol ha-Moëd Pesah, in Rehobot. From the whole of Jewish Palestine, from all the villages, the visitors come. The young people compete with one another in games, athletics, debates, declamations, and song. There is an exhibit of agricultural products after the fashion of a county fair. But what impresses the strangers from abroad most of all is the mighty

chorus of voices raised in the Hebrew songs that have originated on the soil, and have spread to all parts of the land.
Spectators describe the experience as thrilling. Here is the
spirit of play, the token and safeguard of mental health.

Physically the Judean villages are brought close to one
another by a regular omnibus or stage coach system connecting
them with Jaffa, and in Galilee the new wagon roads, imper-
fect though they are, make intercourse between settlements
comparatively easy. Otherwise intercolonial relations have
not been organized. The Waad of each village is independent
of every other. But the subject of a union has not been left
undiscussed. Representatives of the Odessa Committee en-
deavored, in 1903, to effect an organization of the Jewry of
Palestine, at least of the New Settlement, the elements interested in advancing the economic and social status of the
Jews. A Kenessiah, a convention of delegates, assembled at
Zichron Jacob, and steps were taken looking to permanence
and the inclusion eventually of the Old Settlement. Nothing
came of it. Even of sectional unions there is only one, that
of the Judean colonies, organized in 1909, a sort of grange
without the feature of lodge secrets. The general purpose is
the advancement of the economic, cultural, and political situation of the colonies; its specific objects are the founding of
syndicates for the sale of products; the improvement of agricultural methods by the introduction and demonstration of
new implements; the organizing of cattle insurance societies
and the employment of a veterinary surgeon; the improvement of the health conditions in the colonies; the spread of
knowledge by lectures, demonstrations, etc., on agricultural
subjects, and by the introduction of natural science in the

curriculum of the colony schools; and the employment of a professional agronomist who shall supervise agricultural experiments.

Though it cannot be called intercolonial, there is an association that makes itself felt in all the villages, north and south. Ha-Shomer, the Jewish guard or night-watch, is one of the most remarkable phenomena of the new Palestinian life. From the first it was necessary to guard against depredations by the Arabs, and watchmen were engaged from among the suspects to patrol the Jewish fields at night. Though a saving was effected, the arrangement was not calculated to inspire confidence. In point of fact, there were still considerable leakages through favoritism and connivance at thefts; and the Arab guard often was rendered ineffective on account of recurring family and tribal feuds. In the winter of 1909-1910, dissatisfaction with the prevailing system was rife. Especially in the Galilean highland, the nursery of Jewish sentiment from of old, the more ardent spirits among the young workingmen could not brook the humiliation the Jewish farmers had to endure. Word flew from settlement to settlement, and the Jewish colony guard came into existence. At first the service was confined to Galilee; but now practically all the colonies depend upon the Shomerim. Rehobot alone recently organized a watch of its own. Petah Tikwah pays $6000 a year; little Kastinieh's budget shows $268.48 for the item night-watch. A single Shomer receives $100 annually; but as a rule a posse is engaged by the colony as a whole. Two organizations subvention Ha-Shomer, the Odessa Committee and the Workmen's Union. In spite of the costliness of the service, there seems to be hardly a dissenting voice as to its value, a recognition the more remarkable as the citizen, the Baale-Battim, element in the villages still squirms at the idea of a self-constituted and self-governed company of Jewish youths, revolver-armed, most of them noted for zeal and ebullient enthusiasm. That the discharged Arab guard looks upon the Shomerim as "scabs" is not calculated to allay anxiety. The situation offers redoubtable openings on both sides, and there have been a few bloody, even fatal encounters between the two nationalities. The general impression appears to be that the Shomerim are innocent of aggression; they have gone to extremes only in self-defense. Besides insuring the safety of Jewish property, Ha-Shomer has raised the dignity of the Jew in the eyes of his Arab neighbors. A Jew who is a good shot, and rides a horse, bareback if you will, with the same grace as the Arab, and cuts a good figure at that as he gallops 'cross country, exacts respect. At all events, Ha-Shomer with its hundred and more members has become an absolute necessity in Palestine, and a picturesque feature in its rural life. The company is made up of the material needed for the pioneer bands that are to prepare outlying regions through occupancy by themselves for permanent settlement and cultivation by others.

In general, the relation between Jews and Arabs is not unsatisfactory, in spite of the friction that occurs at certain points of contact. The reasonable expectation is that it will improve, because the mutual respect is increasing. The Arab has begun to recognize the value that has accrued to him and the land by the presence and the activity of the Jew. He already pays him the flattery of imitation. In some places he has adopted the modern methods and implements introduced by the Jew. On the other hand, the Jew recognizes that the

Arab may be his teacher in all that relates to the soil. His fiber is, as it were, habituated to it. He knows it by instinct. For instance, the primitive plow of the Arab husbandman, wielded by his predecessor on the soil three thousand years ago, it was thought must be banished beyond recall. More careful investigation has demonstrated that on some soils deep upturning is harmful; the superficial scratching of the wooden plowshare with its small iron attachment is exactly what is needed. Such recognitions, of mutual helpfulness will multiply and make for a better understanding and neighborly tolerance. But that the relation is an aspect of Jewish colonization that will require wisdom and tact and statesmanship can and should not be minimized; nor are the leaders of Palestine public opinion guilty of neglect in this particular.

The Arab is not the only non-Jewish element in the villages. As one goes up and down the land, one constantly meets Gerim, converts to Judaism, from Russia. They have been the special protégées of the ICA. Inured to agricultural labor for centuries, they were doubtless considered a good leaven in the mass of city-bred novices at farming, with whom they were united by one bond—persecution inflicted for the sake of a Panslavic ideal.

About six years ago another element supplying an agricultural leaven was introduced into the colonies, one that tended to fortify Jewish tradition besides. The Yemenites are typically stiffnecked Jews. They claim a history of twenty-four centuries in the Dispersion. Yet they "return" to the Holy Land as inveterately Jewish as though they had never been "exiled" from close communion with the stock of their people. Constituted as they are, tenaciously and loyally

Jewish, intellectually alert, Arabic in speech and habit, accustomed to work in field and shop, they are destined, unless all signs fail, to be a cement between Arab and Jew, between the industrially-minded Jew of the city and the agriculturally-minded Jew of the country, between Sefardi and Ashkenazi.

The above picture of the Jewish village in Palestine is far from complete. Enumerations and descriptions are inadequate to convey its spirit. To learn its flavor one must spend a Sabbath in Zichron Jacob, or Rehobot, or Ekron. It is a Jewish flavor. The spirit of the Sabbath rest descends on the village early Friday afternoon. The laborers hasten home from the fields several hours sooner than on other days. Family groups, decked out in half-Sabbath finery, gather on the porches around the tea urn. Except that the children, released from school earlier than on the ordinary week-day, may be heard singing Hebrew songs as they run in and out of the plantations, an expectant hush lies upon the village. The Sabbath bride is about to arrive. And when she is there, throughout the following day, the place is pervaded by her presence. At the times of rejoicing, Simhat Torah and Purim. all the villagers unite in celebrating them. The festive table is not spread in the houses, but on the open street, and the choruses fill the air. Even those who came from densely-populated Jewish quarters in Polish and Russian cities, or from towns and villages all but entirely Jewish—even they, raised in the atmosphere of a compact Jewish community life, maintain that this is a different Sabbath from any they ever knew. What is the Sabbath spice? Is it the out-of-doors which the Jew has at last recaptured?—the out-of-doors known by his ancestor who sang the Song of Songs?

THE URBAN DEVELOPMENT

" If you want cities, create villages." Doctor Franz Oppenheimer's rule, he himself holds, has been exemplified in Palestine. In 1881 Jerusalem is said to have had 35,000 inhabitants, of whom about 12,000 were Jews; in 1914, 50,000 Jews
out of 100,000 inhabitants were attributed to ·it. Jaffa had
5000 Jews in 1905, by 1910 it had twice five thousand. Haifa
had only 2000 out of 20,000 in 1910, but it has been growing
at a rapid rate since then. The significant point is that the
increase in Jewish city populations corresponds to the development of the rural colonization work.

It was said above that of the 100,000 Jews in Palestine now
(1914), 85,000 are living in twelve cities. They are Jerusalem, Jaffa, Gaza, Hebron, Ramleh, Beer-Sheba, Safed,
Tiberias, Haifa, Saida (Sidon), Accho, and Shefa Amr. The
four " holy cities," Jerusalem, Hebron, Safed, and Tiberias,
contain over 80% of all city-dwelling Jews, and nearly 70% of
all Jews, in Palestine.

These four cities are still the citadels of the Old Settlement.
Yet the new spirit is beginning to make its way even into them.
Considering them either impregnable or negligible, the New

Settlement long made no attempt to woo or to assail them. The immigrant into Palestine that desired to lead a normal city life settled in Jaffa, as the phenomenal growth of its Jewish population shows. Close as we are to our generation's activity, it is impossible to determine whether Old Jerusalem made the advances to the New Settlement, or vice versa. Suffice it to say that the New Settlement has dropped its real or assumed indifference, and that the Holy City has become hospitable to the new, without disavowing its old, ideals.

There was never, of course, any intention on the part of the New Settlement to discredit the religious aspirations of the Old. Its objection was and is to the methods of the Halukkah, the " division " of the moneys gathered from all over the world, wherever Jews dwell, for the support of their brethren leading a life of study and prayer in the Holy Land. On two grounds the religionists claim the support as their right; they consider themselves, as was said before, the " representatives " of the Jews in the Dispersion; and, in so far as they are aged, they receive only that which would have been granted to them had they remained in their communities abroad. As a matter of fact, not all the members of the Old Settlement are advanced in years; nor on the other hand are they all Halukkah recipients. Some are supplied with means by their relatives left behind in Occidental countries; some draw a revenue from their investments in Palestine or in their former homes; some follow a trade or have a business on which they depend, or with which they eke out the small stipend allotted to them in the " division."

Past and present circumstances being what they are, the shrewdest observers of Palestine life hold that what is needed is not the withdrawal of the Halukkah, as the impatient critic insists, but rather its increase, and that it be organized and applied wisely. But a thoroughgoing organization of the Halukkah implies a far-reaching reform " outside of the land " as well as in Palestine: Outside the methods of collection are questionable; inside the methods of distribution.

The Halukkah, it may not be forgotten, has a long history that accounts in part for its blemishes. By some its warrant is sought as far back as the Biblical custom of sending gifts to the Temple at Jerusalem. At all events, from the earliest days of the Dispersion the scattered sons of Israel voluntarily remembered the needs of the remnant in the home-land. Especially the academies were the object of their solicitude. Their contributions, at first a freewill offering, became a tribute, and when saints and scholars " returned " to Palestine, and founded settlements, they sent messengers abroad, to remind the others of the need of their " representatives " and their own duty in the premises. One of them, in the seventeenth century, adduced the example of Christians toward their recluses in Palestine as worthy of imitation by Jews.

This was the beginning of the system of Meshullahim. The messengers confined themselves at first to Turkey and Egypt. In the fifteenth century they went to European countries, their chief centers being London, Amsterdam, Venice, and Leghorn. In the middle of the eighteenth century they extended their operations to the Levant, Germany, France, Russia, Poland, and America. Ezra Stiles in his Diary mentions three in the United States: Moses Malkin in 1759, Hayyim Isaac Karigal in 1771-1773, and Samuel Cohen in 1775. Before the end of another century the relation of the Meshullah to the Palestine community had been put on a definite business basis, and he had added South Africa and

Australia to his bailiwick. But scarcely had he made the
whole Jewish world his sphere, when he began to lose caste.
He came to be regarded widely as the sign of slipshod waste-
fulness and disorganization. That he was at the same time
the symbol of a cosmopolitan outlook, of invincible idealism
on the part of the Jewish masses, and of a Jewish solidarity
that mocked at physical dispersion—this counted for less and
less as more developed means of communication brought the
ends of the earth closer together, and dispelled the glamour
of the Orient that had hung about the person of the messenger.
The " begging letters," one of the developed means of communication substituted for the human messenger, accorded no
better with the modern sense for order. So it came about
that many Jews in Western Europe after 1860 made the
Alliance Israélite Universelle their only Palestine almoners.
It gave public accountings of its funds, a strong recommenda-
tion, even if its undertakings had not been another. That—
an auditing system—is the Halukkah's prime requisite for
the present in the centers of collection.

The distribution of the Halukkah in Palestine has still more
serious aspects. One is tempted to the paradox that it has
never been so disorganizing as when it has set to work to
organize itself. From the thirteenth to the eighteenth century
the collections as well as the semi-annual distributions were
wholly in the hands of the Sefardim. As a means of increasing
their tribute the Ashkenazim separated from the Sefardim.
Alone they could assert more vigorously their claim upon
the support of their former Jewish countrymen, if not on
religious, then on purely charitable grounds. The expedient was successful. The Ashkenazim themselves split
up into groups according to their provenance. Now, after

a hundred years, there are at least thirty Ashkenazic Kolelim, " congregations," some of them consisting of not more than a hundred members, as, for instance, the Kolel of Maramaros, a town in Hungary, and some of even a far smaller number. The Kolelim have their separate systems of collection and distribution, with separate Talmud Torahs, Yeshibot, conventicles or synagogues, and sometimes separate communal institutions, especially congregate houses in which their clients may live rent-free for given periods.

The whole number of Halukkah recipients falls short of 30,000, for whom, it is asserted, the Kolelim have at their disposal $300,000 annually. Other estimates put the figure at $600,000. Either sum compares well with the 10,000 lire reported by the seventeenth-century Meshullah mentioned before. In 1909 the Kolel Galizia alone distributed $63,036. However that may be, the sums are nevertheless not adequate to the need. According to a computation, made in 1912, there are Kolelim that dole out not more than $1.50 a year to their members; in one the annual stipend rises as high as $72. In making the distribution, some take into consideration the number of children in a family, so that no fair average can be struck. Only in the case of three Kolelim, comprising less than 3300 persons, does the individual quota insure even a meager living.

The prevailing system thus necessitates the formation of a new Kolel by arrivals not fortunate enough to have been born in centers already represented by Kolelim, as rigid in their membership requirements as the medieval guild. The Sefardim are shut out entirely from the large Ashkenazic Halukkah system. They have their own still more inadequate Halukkah, drawn from Tripolis, Tunis, Morocco, and Egypt.

Their practice is to distribute the moneys only among their leaders, the Hakamim, and among widows and orphans. And both the Ashkenazic and Sefardic systems disregard the Yemenites, the Persians, and all the small Oriental groups.

It is obvious that organization so understood must lead to injustice, jealousy, recrimination, and pauperization in the worst form, especially when it carries with it largely a system of bookkeeping in Palestine as well as in the centers of collection that disregards the safeguard of publicity. In a word, a healthy, self-reliant, communal development is impossible. The only large urban Palestinian center in which Jewish social life approaches the normal is Jaffa. It is not the only one free from the Halukkah incubus, but being free from it, it is significant that it is the only one in which the Ashkenazic and Sefardic sections form a single community governed by a joint committee.

Leaders of the Halukkah have themselves realized its grave defects. In 1866 a Waad ha-Kelali (Waad kol ha-Kolelim), a Central Committee of the Kolelim, was created, to represent the public interests common to all the Ashkenazim, as well as the interests of those in need of relief who have no Kolel attachment, always barring the Sefardim. For a short period, this Central Committee, acting under pressure with regard to the contributions from America, at that time not represented by a Kolel, did partial justice even to the Sefardim, and in 1885 it introduced a revised system of bookkeeping with public accountings.

The funds from America half a century ago came primarily from two societies, the North American Relief Society for the Indigent Jews of Palestine (incorporated in 1853), and the New York Society for the Relief of the Poor in Palestine.

Their activities were supplemented by general collections. In time the number of American applicants to the Halukkah increased, and after much opposition the American Kolel, Tiferet Yerushalaim, was formed in 1895. The revenues from the United States and Canada all go to the Waad ha-Kelali. It devotes two-thirds to general purposes, and one-third is paid out to the 485 persons comprising the American Kolel. This surprisingly public-spirited arrangement was probably suggested by the circumstance that most of the contributors on this side of the Atlantic are recent immigrants from the centers that support the earlier Kolelim, which ought not to be made to suffer by the accident of a change of habitation on the part of the givers. The amount of the American collection is not known, though there are sure indications that it is large. At all events, the American Kolel is one of the three that grants an income to its members halfway adequate for decent living, though it is not the richest. That distinction belongs to the one called HoD, an abbreviation for Holland-Deutschland (Germany). With the Hungarian Kolel HoD shares another distinction, that of having adopted an improved system, partly of auditing, partly of distribution, partly of general government.

The Waad ha-Kelali has not remained master of the situation even so far as America is concerned. That came about in this way: Kolel lines are drawn to mark not only geographical, but also religious groupings. The HaBaD (the initial letters of the three Hebrew words for wisdom, understanding, and knowledge) is a Hasidic body. The other Ashkenazim are Perushim. Recognizing that immigration had taken a large Hasidic constituency to America, the HaBaD cut loose from the Waad ha-Kelali, and arranged to make independent appeals to the American Jews under what may be described as its jurisdiction. In other words, though Dvinsk, Minsk, and Pinsk, for example, are represented by Kolelim, the Hasidim of these cities pay allegiance to the HaBaD.

The disorganizing influence of the Halukkah affects Tiberias, Safed, and Hebron, with their 20,000 Jews, as it affects Jerusalem with its 50,000. They too have their divisions and subdivisions and separate and multiplied institutions, and the poverty in all is abject.

In picturing the communal situation in Jerusalem—the typical " holy city "—one must not forget that the " division " of funds among their constituencies does not exhaust the activities of the Kolelim. They support Yeshibot, Talmud Torahs, and synagogues; sometimes they have their own—for instance, the Hungarian Kolel has three Yeshibot. They maintain almshouses, which will be dealt with presently. A few have loan societies, one of them specifically for the benefit of mechanics; some provide medical service; one has a clinic; the Kolel Galizia performs the duties of a Hebra Kadisha for the scholars in the community; finally, some assign support to the philanthropic institutions, the hospitals, the orphan asylums, and the Old Folks' Homes. These institutions, however, derive only the smallest part of their income from the Kolelim. Most of it comes direct to them from the outside, either through general collections made specifically for them or from the societies that have founded them, as, for example, is the case with the German hospital Shaare Zedek and the Eye Clinic Le-Maan Zion, both originated and cared for by societies having their seat in Frankfort-on-the-Main. In all it is computed that the revenues of the Old Settlement, its Kolelim and its institutions, reach the sum of $1,000,000 annually.

In Jerusalem there are four hospitals, as many orphan asylums, an insane asylum, two Old Folks' Homes, a blind asylum, and the eye-clinic just mentioned. Jaffa has an inadequate hospital; Haifa a new one, small but well-conducted; Safed has a hospital building, unequipped and therefore unavailable; Hebron is about to replace its small building by one larger and better; Tiberias is wholly destitute of hospital facilities, only comparatively recently the HoD has been stationing physicians and nurses there; finally, several of the colonies have hospital buildings. In Jerusalem the Ashkenazim have their own institutions, and the Sefardim theirs, but neither, nor the two together, can " compete " with the opportunities offered by the missionaries. Not a single one of their institutions—they are all indispensable—is equal to the legitimate calls made upon it. Most of them are unsatisfactory as to equipment and administration; and if the appointments in one or another meet the requirements of science and humanity, it is sure not to be sufficiently endowed to take in as many applicants as its space permits. There is not one that is not a monument to the selfless devotion of one or many individuals, and there is not one that is not struggling under a burden of accumulated debt or a lamentably insufficient income.

The oldest charity in Jerusalem is the Kuppat-Tamhui, a public kitchen. For reasons growing out of conditions in the city and in the land the distribution of free meals is fundamentally a necessary institution. Many of the schools, the Talmud Torahs and some of the modern institutions as well, provide them for their pupils. Along this line the most notable contribution to Palestinian charity in latter years has been made from America, in the Nathan Straus Soup Kitchen, or Relief Station, which, since 1912, has been dispensing food daily, including Matzot at Passover, to from four to five hundred of the old, the feeble, and the sick folk of Jerusalem. The utility of this work has been demonstrated particularly since the war cut Palestine off from the revenues usually flowing into the land from Central Europe and Russia. It is reported that since last August the usual number of beneficiaries of the Straus Soup Kitchen has been increased to at least a thousand a day.

Another recent undertaking is the Visiting Nurses' Settlement of the American Women's Zionist organization Hadassah. It has established a midwives' service, enabling Jewish women to refrain from resorting to the English Missionary Hospital, the only maternité in Jerusalem. Besides, its two nurses and several caretakers are detailed for duty in nineteen schools, to look after the general health of the pupils, more particularly to take care of their eyes, by way of supplementing the work of the Le-Maan Zion Eye Clinic, whose physician directs the examinations for trachoma and other eye diseases in the schools; and general district nursing is done by them at the Settlement and in all parts of the city under the direction of the physician of the Rothschild Hospital. The organization is supported by groups of men and women in Chicago and Pittsburgh as well as by its own Zionist branches, and that it could put its plans into operation in Jerusalem and have two nurses at work there at the time when this came about, was due to the personal co-operation and the substantial support of Mr. and Mrs. Nathan Straus, who, besides, fitted up the Settlement House in Jerusalem. The ultimate object of the Society is the establishment of a Nurses' Training School.

When the New Settlement arrived in the "eighties," the Jerusalem they came to was to all intents and purposes the city described above. A few of the charitable institutions enumerated have been founded since then, and a few Kolelim have sprung up, but on the whole the communal traditions were fixed. Occupied with the complexities of its own situation, the New Settlement could not be expected to tackle the older abuses. In one respect, however, it was forced to take immediate action, but there, it happens, the Old Settlement had done preliminary work, in which an American had an initial share.

Nothing in Palestine, in city or in country, has been more serious than the housing problem, and that seems to have been understood or divined by Judah Touro, the American philanthropist, who died in 1854. In his will, he left a sum of $60,000 as a trust fund for the erection of almshouses in Jerusalem. The trust was administered by Sir Moses Montefiore and the North American Relief Society for the Indigent Jews of Jerusalem. This explains why the group of twenty or more dwellings to the southwest of Jerusalem is known as the "Montefiore Almshouses," instead of by Judah Touro's name.

The noteworthy implications are that nearly sixty years ago it should have been discerned that a fundamental need was dwellings for the Jews, and that the trustees of Judah Touro's bequest should have had the sagacity and perhaps the boldness to build the hospices beyond the walls that mark the boundaries of the Inner City, several miles away from the specific Jewish quarter. This original "Montefiore Colony," with its windmill making it a landmark, has remained all but an isolated group on the Hebron road. But on the

Jaffa road, leading westward from the city, and to the north beyond the Damascus Gate, Jewish " colony " after Jewish " colony " has arisen, until the Jewish city beyond the walls is three times as large as the city within the walls.

To know what this expansion means one must have been in the dark courts within courts, with their cave-like, windowless dwellings, in the Maghrebi (Moroccan) quarter in the Inner City, or in the underground chambers in Tiberias into which men and women and their children and their herds of goats disappear together as night falls.

The " Montefiore Colony " pointed the way in two directions. The almshouse idea was taken up by the Kolelim. Many of them have built and now maintain congregate houses or hospices. The HaBaD has nine in different parts of the city; the Grodno Kolel has two, one in the city, one beyond the walls. In most instances the regulation is that a family may occupy one of these " cells " rent-free for a period of three years. Then it must vacate the little shelter to make room for another applicant. The wealthier Kolelim build separate houses, grouped together in one locality : the Warsaw Kolel has 68 such houses, the Hungarian 240. In most instances the Kolelim have received special donations for the purpose. Three Americans, Marks Nathan, of Chicago, Moses Alexander and Moses M. Vodner, of New York, are responsible the first for 50 houses, the second for 20, and the third for 20.

There are, in addition, other " colonies," which are wholly independent of the Kolelim and of charity. They antedate the New Settlement, but they have multiplied greatly with it and through it. The largest and one of the earliest of this type is Meah Shearim, " the hundred-gated," begun in 1860. A group of a hundred men formed an association with dues of

about $40 annually; land was bought and ten houses built
each year. As soon as ten were ready for occupancy they were
assigned to the members by lot. Those provided with houses
paid rent amounting to 20% of their former annual contribution, while the rest continued to pay the full quota. After
all were housed, the surplus was used for public improvements,
for keeping the streets in repair, building a synagogue and
bath, but particularly erecting a wall around the Settlement,
the gates of which were locked at night—an indication of the
danger of living outside of the walls in those days. The
original hundred tenants have been more than doubled, and
the Meah Shearim mutual building association has had many
imitators. Later on the idea was taken up as a business
venture, and speculation in land and buildings became rife.

Similar to Meah Shearim are the four " colonies "—a mis-
nomer that has established itself in Palestinian parlance—that
have been built with the aid of the Testimonial Fund to Sir
Moses Montefiore, which at his urgence was devoted to public
works for the improvement of the condition of the Jews in
the Holy Land. Its revenues have been applied partly as a
loan fund to the purpose of house-building. A non-interest
bearing loan is granted to a building association, the amount
varying in proportion to the association's own capital. The
loan is to be returned in fifteen years, the first installment being
payable in five years. In its time the Anglo-Palestine Bank
entered the field on somewhat the same plan, and earlier the
ICA on its own account put up workingmen's houses primarily
for the employees of the Alliance weaving establishment. The
ICA " colony," called Nahalat Zion, first contemplated thirty
houses; the great number of applicants compelled an enlarge-
ment of the plan. The tenants are given the chance of becom

ing the owners on easy terms. Naturally all such colonies are
provided with cisterns, a sewer system, and other public improvements. A second quarter, Nahalat Zadok, erected by the
ICA, on a different plan, has in view business men as tenants.

Another sort of "colonies" owes its existence to the
tendency of Jews from one or another city or country to flock
together. Thus arose the various Yemenite quarters, the
Persian quarter, sometimes referred to as the Tin Quarter,
a part of the building material being Standard Oil Company's
cans, the Urfali quarter, and the only handsome one, the
Bokhara quarter, in which there are "residences" built as
wealth and taste dictate.

In Jaffa the housing-problem was equally acute. Here the
Sefardic Jews had exercised foresight. Long ago they went
forth from the two Jewish quarters of the town, and secured
plots on the sandy shores of the Mediterranean. 'Their pru-
dence has been rewarded. After the opening of the Jaffa-
Jerusalem road in 1892, the city spread phenomenally. In
1881 there had been 10,000 inhabitants; in 1892, 23,000, and
at present their number exceeds 60,000. Rents leaped higher
and higher. A co-operative building association was formed
by Jews in 1906. Nothing was done until, in 1909, the
National Fund, making another departure from its original
policy, extended a loan of $48,000 to the Ahuzat Bayyit. As
though by magic there grew up a Jewish suburb, Tel-Abib,
of which a traveler writes: "I must confess that I have not
seen anywhere in the Orient (including Cairo) so healthy,
dustless, trim, and beautiful a quarter. . . . . It owes its
existence to money and organizing talent. It is Hebrew all
the way through, and it is amazing to see the self-possession
of these hitherto cowed Russian Jews. The erect carriage

of the younger generation is admirable. Their melancholy expression is disappearing. One sees handsome, gay people, enthusiastic and industrious. The children were frolicking on the streets, in masks—it was Purim." . . . .

Tel-Abib is a wholly Jewish suburb shut off from traffic from sundown on Friday to sundown on Saturday. The streets are lined with trees, the water supply is ample, the concrete houses are square-set and surrounded by garden plots, and the public improvements are modern. With the city of Jaffa twenty minutes off, the suburb by the sea is connected by means of an omnibus, running every ten minutes. Many of the public buildings of the Jaffa Jewish community are there: the great schools, the Palestine Office, and the office of the Odessa Committee, and others are contemplated: a synagogue, a hospital, a hotel, and a Jewish " city-hall," for the transaction of all matters of business between the Turkish Government and the Jewish community. The chief official that conducts the Governmental business is called mukhtar, as in the colonies. Hitherto his functions have been confined to dealings with the Jews of Ottoman citizenship, but since the system of Capitulations has been abrogated, his sphere must be considerably larger. And if Ottomanization increases among Jews as heretofore, a community like that of Tel-Abib will soon, under the Turkish administrative system, have its own Mayor and large liberties in municipal regulation. For its internal affairs, Tel-Abib has a Waad of seven, chosen at a general assembly of all the residents, whether owners of houses or lots or only tenants, provided they have rented and occupied two rooms and a kitchen for at least a year. There are considerably more than a thousand residents, and the budget for 1913 was $3618.

Tel-Abib has not appeased the house-hunger of the Jaffa Jews. The gymnasium has drawn to the city a large number of Russian Jews who desire to give their children an education. They clamor for dwellings almost as insistently as the Yemenites. Already a second quarter, Nahalat Benjamin, has been undertaken for artisans, clerks, and merchants. It is adjacent to Tel-Abib, and again the National Fund has extended credit to the builders. The criticism has been made that the conditions of the contracts between the members of the building association and the National Fund operating through the bank have not been sufficiently exacting. Though Tel-Abib is handsome and hygienically constructed, it is so by a happy accident. The critics of the National Fund desire truly " restricted suburbs," in which the loan-extending body shall take upon itself the functions of a municipality, regulating the width of the streets, the height of the houses, the construction of the drainage system, etc. Above all there has been adverse criticism on the score of the National Fund's having omitted to determine the time within which houses should be erected on the plots acquired with its loans. The result of the omission is that some of the building lots have remained unimproved, and the land has risen to three or four times its first value. Thus the National Fund has aided its clients, not to secure a home, which was its object, but to make a snug profit through speculation, while many would-be residents had perforce to be turned away.

A second building association, operating under private auspices, contemplates a quarter on land bought from the Geulah. Its plan is to connect Tel-Abib with the two old Jewish quarters in Jaffa proper. The buildings will be constructed for business purposes, with a view to the need of merchants.

Finally, in 1913, work was begun in the suburb Hebrah Hadashah, close to Tel-Abib, with its main street to run along the Mediterranean shore.

The "restricted suburb" idea may be realized in Haifa, where the quarter Herzelia has been started on the side of Carmel by the building association Ahawat Ahim. It purchased its land from the Real Estate Company Palästina, a share company with rigid regulations. Parcels of land, if not improved within a stated period, may be bought back by the company on stipulated terms. The owners of lots must agree to contribute to certain public expenditures, as police, water, sewer, illumination, streets, park, and taxes. The height of the houses and their other dimensions are limited, and their place is defined in relation to the street. The purchaser undertakes not to maintain a factory, shop, or store on his premises, and to build his outhouses with due regard to cleanliness and health. In case of sale, the Real Estate Company has the first option, and if it does not exercise it, and the house and lot are sold to a third party, he must be made to accept the regulations agreed to by the original owner, or the sale is invalid.

Herzelia is well under way. Some of the houses were completed a few years ago, and no sooner finished than they were occupied. It has a Jewish hotel, too, one of the desiderata in all the Jewish centers in Palestine.

Soon Jerusalem will have in addition to its "colonies" a modern suburb, like Haifa's Herzelia and Jaffa's Tel-Abib, Nahalat Benjamin, Shaarayim, and Hebrah Hadashah. Steps have already been taken to build it. Then Safed and Tiberias will not be able to resist long. The modern spirit will pierce to them and make of them abodes worthy of the charms that nature has conferred upon them—the one perched high in rugged Galilee, the other set on the shores of the azure, hill-girt Harp-Lake.

If Tiberias refuses to follow the example set by her sister "holy city" Jerusalem, her stubbornness will have to yield to the changes encroaching upon her borders. Already a motor boat plies between the town at the northwestern end of the Sea and Semakh, the railroad station of the Haifa-Damascus Rail-road at the southern end. The same railroad is about to throw out a branch southward from Merhawiah, and connect Haifa with Nablus and Jerusalem. Not far from Semakh is the National Fund Farm Kinneret, one part of which is a peninsula extending into the Jordan, the site of the ancient city of Tarichaea. There, at Kerak, the Palestine Land Development Company is planning a winter resort. In twenty minutes by motor boat, the visitors may reach the hot springs lying on the western shore of the Sea south of Tiberias, between it and Kinneret. To the north, opposite Kerak, across the Sea, and beyond the Upper Galilean hills and the Lebanon range, rises the snow-capped Hermon, while all around a tropical vegetation grows rank. From the ten or more Galilean colonies milk, eggs, butter, poultry, and vegetables can easily be brought, not only to the tourists at Kerak, but also to the puny babies at Tiberias in the dark, slimy, vaulted streets or in the cave-like chambers below the level of the street. When Tiberias was founded, it was declared unclean, because it was the site of a cemetery. It became later the synonym for the study and the interpretation of the law; the seat of legend hallowed by the memory of Rabbi Meïr Baal ha-Ness; the reputed burial-place of great scholars; and the refuge of saints and mystics. To-day its heritage is, besides the Halukkah collected in the Rabbi Meïr Baal ha-Ness "pushkes," only malaria and misery; it is unclean because it is in the clutches of dire poverty. The currents of the young Palestinian Jewish life should soon gather impetus enough to sweep away all this hideousness, and in restoring beauty and charm to their own revitalize the traditions of the place into modern motive forces.

The housing problem shares the place of prime importance in the Palestinian cities with the problem of creating opportunities for work. The retail business is naturally restricted. In Jaffa and Haifa many of the shops on the main streets are in Jewish hands. In Jerusalem there are stationers, druggists, clothing, dry goods, and linen merchants, dealers in building materials (largely cement in recent years), booksellers, dealers in olive wood and other souvenirs, and of course dealers in Jewish religious articles. There are also five insurance offices and several private banks.

To the Alliance Israélite Universelle belongs the credit for having taken the first effective step towards the introduction of handicrafts. As early as 1882 it opened a well-equipped and adequately subsidized trade school in Jerusalem, for carpentry, cabinet-making, wood-carving, weaving, dyeing, machine construction, and all sorts of smithies—blacksmithing, coppersmithing, and locksmithing. The object was to train apprentices, and its success has been admirable so far as the manual skill of its graduates is concerned. Unfortunately the spirit that sent so many of the pupils of the Alliance Agricultural School at Mikweh Israel out of Palestine, prevailed here too, and with the same deplorable result. The girls' industrial school was of more benefit to the community, though the hair net industry, dressmaking, and embroidery, the subjects taught, afford only a pittance.

The next attempt at industrial training was not made for nearly a quarter of a century. In the interval there had been great progress. Mr. Boris Schatz, in his Bezalel School for arts and crafts, keeps his eye constantly on the land and the material he has to deal with. The consequence is that instead of exporting trained men, he exports goods. He teaches carpet-weaving, filigree silver work, beaten copper and brass work, ivory carving, lithography, lace-making, and other related subjects. In a few years his school, which is built on National Fund land and with the assistance of the National Fund, occupied 430 persons, who earned, in 1912, $27,000 in wages, while the sale of the products amounted to $50,000. Their work, as in the Alliance school, is sold, the Society backing Mr. Schatz's efforts having succeeded in securing a market for his wares in a number of the large European centers. In the school building there are two Jewish museums, one of Jewish antiquities and art objects, the other a collection of the flora and fauna of Palestine, the only natural history museum in Palestine proper. To these two museums the pupils are taught to resort for the motives to be elaborated in their work. In both schools a beneficial change has recently been made, by which the educational undertaking is separated from the industrial. The Bezalel Workshops, Ltd., is to be conducted wholly on a commercial basis.

It will be recalled that the Bezalel co-operated with the National Fund in establishing an industrial colony at Ben Shamen, where twelve families of Yemenites are securing a livelihood by means of truck-farming as well as filigree work and carpet-weaving. So also in Jerusalem the Bezalel has introduced home industries. Carpet-weaving is done at the homes of some of the workers, and the needle lace peculiar to the Orient at others. For the introduction of the latter, not only in Jerusalem, but also in Jaffa, Safed, and Tiberias, credit is due to the Verband jüdischer Frauen für Kulturarbeit in Palästina. About four hundred girls are engaged in the industry, earning from forty to seventy-five cents a week, and the most skilled forty cents a day. The same needle lace, together with embroidery, dressmaking, and plain sewing, is taught also at the Evelina de Rothschild School, and in the Alliance Girls' Schools throughout the country.

In the Bezalel filigree and copper and brass workshops, as well as in the Alliance weaving establishment, Yemenites are employed in large numbers. Here as in the colonies they are docile, skillful, and industrious. They bring artisan habits with them from Arabia; there too they were carpenters, masons, blacksmiths, goldsmiths, tanners, metal workers, and shoe-makers. It is the merit of a Christian woman, Mrs. Finn, the widow of the sometime British Consul to Jerusalem, to have been the first to find work for the quick fingers of the Yemenites. On her beautiful property close to Jerusalem called Abraham's Vineyard, she has been employing Yemenites since first they came to Palestine, in the quarry there and in the little olive soap factory. By the way it should be noted that some of the masonry work in Palestine is done by Jews, especially by the Yemenites.

The idea of industrial opportunity and industrial training has taken root. Mr. Nathan Straus established, in 1913, in connection with his Relief Station, workshops for unskilled persons. They were taught to make mother-of-pearl beads, a profitable industry up to that time carried on exclusively by the people of Bethlehem, who had guarded the secret of their manufacture jealously. From beads the step was taken to the making of pearl buttons, which appeal to a larger market than that created by the tourist. The shop gives work to a considerable number of the unemployed. The hope is that the undertaking will in time be self-supporting.

The women of the Ezrat Nashim Society of Jerusalem have opened industrial and domestic training classes for girls; and in Safed the B'nai B'rith established a manual training school.

Three other attempts at industrial training should be mentioned more explicitly, because they are the creations of the Halukkah circles on their own behalf. In Jaffa, in 1906, a handicrafts school, Bet Melakah, was organized by an orthodox society, Shomre Torah, for youths of indifferent endowment and taste for Talmud study. Besides the lessons in the iron-forge and the carpenter's shop, they are taught drawing, mathematics, physics, etc., and only a few hours a day are devoted to the Talmud. The school has manufactured large and expensive iron pieces of workmanlike character. Jerusalem followed the example of Jaffa. In 1908, the HoD established the Darke Hayyim, a manual trade school on the same lines as the Jaffa school. Finally, the Mahaseh le-Yetomim, better known as the Diskin Orphanage, a Kolel institution in every sense and implication of the word, has opened three classes, for tailoring, shoemaking, and Torah-writing. This is the application of Halukkah funds that friends of Palestine now have in mind, and that should go hand in hand with their increase, if the blot on Palestine life is ever to be wiped off. As one writer phrases it, " The Halukkah must help to abolish the Halukkah."

The ICA also has made a small contribution to the industrial development of Jerusalem, by furnishing knitting machines on easy terms, and a large contribution, by establishing a loan bank for merchants and artisans. The figures for 1911 relative to the latter are instructive: On January 1, there were 501 borrowers on its books; of these 143 paid up wholly by the end of the year their indebtedness of $5248. In the meantime there were 170 new borrowers, who, with the 358 left over, owed the bank $22,271.76. Of the 170 new borrowers, 86 were Ashkenazim, 48 Sefardim, and 36 Yemenites, 63 being merchants, as against 107 artisans.

What could have been the trades of these one hundred and seven artisans? According to the report of the French consul for 1907-1908, quoted by Mr. Nawratzki, there were six thousand Jewish workmen in Jerusalem: joiners, masons, painters, cobblers, tailors, turners, printers, bookbinders, millers, weavers, goldsmiths, watchmakers, saddlers, wagon-builders, mattress-makers, carvers, paperhangers, coppersmiths, Sefer Torah scribes, etc. Their wages, the reporter maintains, ranged from ten cents a day for glaziers to $1.50 for masons, weavers, and founders.

In the country at large there are various industries in Jewish hands, but all conducted on a small scale: In Artuf oil is extracted from the thyme that grows wild there; the Petah Tikwah experiment with geraniums has been mentioned; in other colonies the castor oil plant is cultivated for commercial purposes, and oil is extracted from sesame and olives. In Jaffa, in Jerusalem, in Beer-Sheba, the last only lately beginning to attain to importance, there are mills in Jewish hands. Jaffa has a machine shop, a furniture factory, a tannery, and motor works. In Haifa there is a foundry. Near Ramleh a Jew has a lime-kiln. The wine and cognac industry of the colonies has been described. Connected with it is the manufacture of the barrels needed, as the manufacture of boxes goes with the orange industry. The dairy industries are growing.   Safed is delivering cheese to Haifa and to Jerusalem.   The Lower Galilean colonies are sending all kinds of dairy products to Haifa.   Recently, when, on account of conditions incidental to the war, Daganiah on the Sea of Tiberias was cut off from its market at Haifa, the colonists adjusted themselves quickly to the situation.   Instead of using the railroad westward from Semakh, they used it eastward, and transported the stock on hand to Damascus.

These are outward signs of normality.   That there is an inner rapprochement between the two Settlements auguring well for an undivided communal life rests upon many intangible manifestations.   Formerly the " dying colony " was only a thorn in the side of the New Settlement.   It is now prepared to admit that without the deep religious enthusiasm of its predecessor, the progress it is proud of, costly as it has been in respect of every form of human devotion, might have required a thousand times more sacrifices.   It recognizes that the Old Settlement has performed the valuable service of linking the New Settlement with the Jewish past in the Jewish land, just as for centuries it had performed the other valuable service of linking the Jewries of the world with one another through the Jewish land.   The Old Settlement, in turn, is relenting towards the method and content of modern instruction.   Excommunications are not so frequent as formerly.   The Kolelim themselves are encouraging trade education instead of threatening the withdrawal of the Halukkah from those whose children follow a secular occupation.   Rabbi M. Lerner, of Altona, has organized the Moriah " for the promotion of the agricultural colonization of Palestine on an orthodox religious basis." The Old Settlement realizes that its cherished object, intense Jewishness in life and thought, is not subserved by forcing all its youths to the Talmudic studies for which many are not fitted. Above all it is conceded, even by some who are concerned officially, that the Halukkah, the source of most of the friction, stands in need of reform, and the existence of the Mizrahi party within the Zionist movement is a guarantee of future co-operation and amalgamation between the two sections of the community.

There have been signs of progress even in the matter of centralized organization. As was mentioned before, the Jaffa community is a unit. Sefardim and Ashkenazim act together. In Jerusalem, a few years ago, the collapse of one of the largest charitable institutions produced an acute crisis in communal affairs. The Waad ha-Kelali saw an opportunity in favor of compacter organization. It appointed an executive committee, a Waad ha-Ir, a city council. The move turned out to be premature, chiefly because the new body had no funds to apportion, as had been contemplated. But even the failure is instructive as an indication of the temper of the leaders. During the still acuter crisis produced by the present war, if the reports that have reached the outside world suffice as a basis for inferences, Jerusalem has learnt the need of a centralized life. Bitter necessity may be welding the community into a unit. To be sure, even though the immediate effect of hardships be as satisfactory as described, it would be rash to jump to the conclusion that the Kolel barriers are down for always. The report is adduced only to show the trend that does actually exist toward unified Jewish action.

THE CULTURAL DEVELOPMENT

Important Place of Palestine Cultural Development—Talmud
Torahs—Lämel School—Modernized Talmud Torahs—Hebrew
as the Language of Instruction—Hebrew in the Villages—
Alliance Israélite Universelle—Evelina de Rothschild School
—Hilfsverein der deutschen Juden: Kindergartens—Second-
ary Schools—Higher Education—Higher Education in Jaffa—
Mizrahi School: Tahkemoni—Two New Settlement Schools
in Jerusalem—Jewish Institute for Technical Education—
Zionist Hebrew Schools—The Yeshibot—Teachers' Union—
Libraries—Conservatories of Music—The Press—Publication
Societies—Propaganda for Sanitation—Jerusalem Water
Supply.

Since time immemorial " dry " masonry has been in vogue in
Palestine. Wieldy blocks of the various kinds of stone, chalky
and basalt, quarried in the country are piled upon and next
to one another, with no sort of cement between them. The
method is still employed, particularly for inclosures. Rural
colonization, urban economic progress, industries, philan-
thropies, are such a dry-masonry structure of Palestinian
life. The mortar is supplied by its intellectual manifestations.

First and most important naturally is the educational system
in the restricted pedagogic sense.

The Yeshibot and the Talmud Torahs are as old as the Palestinian Jewish Settlement itself. In a sense they are the
raison d'être of its existence. Jewish lore and research were
to have a home peculiarly their own. The Kolelim stint their
members to maintain the schools. They go further; they establish new ones in the face of the poverty of their constituents.
There is hardly a choice in the matter. As the outlying " colonies " spring up, miles distant from the Inner City, they must
be provided with school facilities. The Halukkah supporters
abroad abet the Kolelim in this purpose with at least as much
effectiveness as in their relief work. But the zeal and the need

of the Kolelim outstrip the interest or the means of those to whom they appeal, for no cry from Palestine comes so insistently as the cry for funds for the Yeshibot and the Talmud Torahs.

Of Talmud Torahs there are in Jerusalem nine, with from three to four thousand pupils, taught by upwards of one hundred and fifty teachers. The Sefardim have their own, the oldest of all; the Perushim among the Ashkenazim have theirs, the largest of all, one with eight branches in as many " colonies "; since 1886 the Hasidim have one, and so have the Maghrebim, the Persians, the Yemenites, the Bokharans, and the Grusinians. The Sefardic is the only one that deviates from the curriculum of the usual type of Talmud Torah. It adds Turkish, Arabic, and arithmetic to the Jewish religious branches. The language of instruction is Yiddish in the German institutions, Ladino, or Spagniol, in the Sefardic, and Persian and Arabic in the others. Recently one of the Sefardic schools has adopted Hebrew. The guess may be hazarded that the sum total of the income of all together does not exceed $35,000.

According to Nawratzki, there are in Jaffa 8 such Talmud Torahs; in Hebron, 4; in Haifa, 1; in Tiberias, 2; and in Safed, 4; with 1380 pupils and 71 teachers.

The first protest against the system of instruction espoused by the Talmud Torah, which denied absolutely the need of even the most rudimentary secular education, was the Lämel School (1856), mentioned in the introduction to this article. The school was excommunicated by the Ashkenazic leaders, but it received a warm welcome from the Sefardim, to whom its European equipment must have made it a children's Paradise after their Arab Kuttab, lacking light physically and method

spiritually. For over thirty years the Sefardim availed themselves of the opportunities it offered. Then, much depleted in
attendance, it was attached for a short time to the orphan
asylum founded by Frankfort Jews, and in 1911 it passed
under the jurisdiction of the Hilfsverein der deutschen Juden
as its Jerusalem boys' school.

The protest embodied in the Lämel School entered Jerusalem from the outside. Ten years later, in 1866, something in
the nature of a revolt from the inside brought about the establishment of the Bet ha-Midrash Doresh Zion, known in Jerusalem, from its founder, as the Blumenthal School. It had
two peculiarities, one pedagogic, the other fiscal. It made the
study of a European language compulsory, and it had a sinking
fund to draw upon. The revolt fared no better than the protest: excommunication by the Ashkenazim, acceptance and use
by the Sefardim. Since 1911 the school is under the direction
of the HoD. The change of management will probably bring
it into line with the educational policy of the Freie Verein-
igung für die Interessen des orthodoxen Judentums. This
Frankfort organization has been operating in the Holy Land
since 1909. It maintains an educational director, and has
established Talmud Torah schools in Petah Tikwah, Rishon
le-Zion, Ekron, Katra, and Haifa, in some of these places
supplanting former institutions of the kind, in others add-
ing a second to the one existing before. Besides these boys'
schools it has girls' schools in Petah Tikwah and Ekron, the
former equipped with the domestic training outfit described in
a previous section. Its system of schools aims to keep in view
modern Palestinian needs; the pupils are even given a modi-
cum of agricultural training; the pedagogic methods are up-
to-date; it has put up several suitable school buildings; and it

conducts a teachers' course at Petah Tikwah, which is the seat of the director.

The Hilfsverein der deutschen Juden is also contributing to the inner reform of the Talmud Torah in contrast to the laissez-faire policy once thought inevitable. For the purpose it is subsidizing two Talmud Torahs, one at Hebron, the other, the Grusinian, at Jerusalem. In the latter it had the co-operation of the Odessa Committee. The curriculum has been modernized by the introduction of Arabic and arithmetic, and the religious subjects are taught systematically.

In the new Talmud Torahs of the Frankfort Society and in those supported by the Hilfsverein the language of instruction is Hebrew. With its adoption they ranged themselves among the forces that are determining the new order in Palestine, for the new order is committed irrevocably to Hebrew as the Jewish vernacular. Every modern educational agency has come to acknowledge this, and has modified its program accordingly.

After a quarter of a century the Alliance Israélite Universelle took up the innovation represented by the Lämel School. In its elementary and secondary schools, it unhappily committed the same mistake as at Mikweh Israel and in its Technical School. They were not redolent of the soil. The most crying evil that resulted was a deplorable confusion pedagogically speaking. A fundamental difficulty in the East is the multiplicity of languages. The child spends so much time and effort in acquainting itself with the media of education, that it rarely reaches the substance. The linguistic attainments of the Levantine are held up to admiration, but they have their drawbacks. With Arabic as the language of the land, and Turkish the official language, the problem in Palestine is at best difficult. The Alliance drew the Gordian knot still tighter by making French the language of instruction in the schools. The fashion was set for modern outside agencies. When the Anglo-Jewish Association, in 1898, took over the Evelina de Rothschild School, the medium became English, and when the Hilfsverein came into the land at the beginning of the century, it gave a prominent place to German. It is all the more signifi- cant of the current of events that nevertheless each of these successive agencies allotted more and more time to Hebrew than its predecessor. The Evelina de Rothschild laid greater stress upon it than the Alliance, and the Hilfsverein more than co-ordinated it with German. Even the Alliance has had to modify its scheme, though, to be sure, it is the subven- tion of the Odessa Committee that maintains a number of its Hebrew teachers.

Meantime the people were deciding the language question in their own way. Circumstances forced the colonists to conduct their schools on the simplest basis. The teachers came not from France, or England, or Germany, but from Russia. It was conceivable that a French or an English or a German Jew should press his language upon Palestine as a culture-bearer. For the Russian Jew to do the same was unthinkable. In Russia the study of Hebrew for living purposes had been inher- ited from the illuminati, the Maskilim, of the early nineteenth century. The events of 1881-1882 and of 1891, and the rise of the Palestinian colonization projects, had only intensified love of the ancient holy language. The country school teachers would instinctively have taught Jewish children in Palestine in Hebrew, even if the New Settlement had not put Hebrew upon its banner. From the first it had revolted against the confusion of tongues in Jewish Palestine. Hebrew naturally was the only compromise acceptable to all the Jewish " nationals." And no indulgence was permitted. The parole was one language and only one pronunciation, the native Sefardic. For some it was more painful to sacrifice the off-color of the Hebrew vowels than to renounce the language they had spoken from their birth, though for the older people this too must have been far from easy. Many a social group adopted the rule of imposing a fine upon its members when in the heat of discussion they slipped from Hebrew into German, Yiddish, French, or Russian.

Hebrew was thus the only possibility in the public schools of Palestine. In the villages Arabic was inevitable, and so even in the colony schools two languages had to be taught; all others were banished from the curriculum of the elementary school. Petah Tikwah alone of all the villages still clings to the French inherited from the Rothschild "administration." Where the village school develops from primary to secondary grades, a European language, French or German, is added, but it is distinctly put into the category of foreign languages.

Once the language question is dismissed, only benefit accrued to Palestine from the presence of the Alliance, the Anglo-Jewish Association, and the Hilfsverein. The Alliance planted centers of light in Jerusalem, Jaffa, Haifa, Safed, Tiberias, and Saida, providing everywhere except in Jaffa for girls as well as boys, and everywhere except in Saida in separate schools, and everywhere attaching manual training features to the classes, especially in the girls' schools.

The Evelina de Rothschild School, only for girls, of whom it enrolls 650 at a time, teaching them handicrafts and training them for domestic work, has the distinction of having won the confidence and good-will of all the elements of the Ashkenazim, the Sefardim, and the other Orientals, with the exception only of the extremists that remain wholly unreconciled to secular education.

The Hilfsverein with its veritable network of schools has a variety of educational achievements to its credit. None exceeds in importance the establishment of Kindergartens, three in Jerusalem, three in Jaffa, and one each in Rehobot, Safed, Haifa, and Tiberias—an undertaking the value of which is enhanced by the exclusive use of Hebrew in all. The innovation was recognized as an indispensable adjunct to the Palestinian educational system. The Alliance and the Evelina de Rothschild followed suit. The devotion and heroism of the Kindergartners cannot be appreciated unless one pauses to take in the picture presented by a Palestinian Kindergarten: Yiddish and Spagniol-speaking toddlers, by the side of the Adjami babies lisping their Persian, the Grusinians with their Russian, and Urfali, Maghrebi, Yemenite, and Aleppo tots with their various dialects of Arabic—this babel to be reduced to Sefardic Hebrew by a Russian or German teacher!

In point of secondary education, the Hilfsverein supplemented the Alliance, in Jerusalem with a girls' and a boys' school, the latter being the Lämel Foundation; with a boys' school in Jaffa; and with a school for both sexes in Haifa and in the colony of Katra.

That is not yet all. In addition to its primary and secondary schools, and its contributions to agricultural training in the colonies noted before, the Hilfsverein made admirable provision for the higher education. It has a course for Kindergarten teachers; a seminary for rabbis, calculated particularly for the Sefardic population; and a teachers' seminary founded in 1904. The candidates are expected to take a course in agriculture to fit them for teaching in the village schools. The seminary has already supplied elementary teachers to some of the Hilfsverein schools, and attached to it is a commercial college with four classes. The language of instruction in all these higher institutions is German, though Hebrew is of course a prominent feature in the curriculum. These, all of them in Jerusalem, with evening extension or continuation classes for adults, form a remarkably complete system. In round numbers the Hilfsverein taught 3,000 pupils, and its force consisted of 150 teachers.

The impetus to adopt Hebrew as the sole and only medium of instruction issuing from the village school, bore fruit in secondary and higher education, first in Jaffa and then in Jerusalem. Jaffa, the mother city of the Judean colonies, had indeed kept even pace with the colonies. In 1892 a boys' school, Bet ha-Sefer be-Jaffa, was founded, supported by the Odessa Committee and subventioned by the B'nai B'rith of America. It is now the school of the Alliance. The girls' school, Bet Sefer la-Banot, followed in 1893. In both schools Hebrew was the language. With the seminary for women teachers lately attached to it, the Bet Sefer la-Banot continues to be subsidized by the Odessa Committee, which is bound by a resolution, fathered by Ahad Ha-Am, to devote more than one-fourth of its revenues to education in Palestine. It has seven classes, and its 500 pupils, Ashkenazim, Sefardim, and Yemenites, are housed in a beautiful building, the gift of a Russian-Jewish well-wisher from Irkutsk. It is fitted out with all the appointments of a modern school building, and set in a large tree-planted playground.

Most important of all from the point of view of an eventual system of Hebrew education in Palestine was the founding, in 1907, of the Theodor Herzl Hebrew Gymnasium, with seven classes, exclusive of the three preparatory classes. The curriculum is patterned after the German gymnasium, and the pupils graduated from it are prepared to enter a German, French, or Swiss university. As in all the other schools mentioned there is a tuition fee, and the moderate revenue thus derived is supplemented by the Odessa Committee and by the contributions of Jews the world over, America, Europe, and South Africa. This gymnasium also has a worthy building for its more than seven hundred pupils, boys and girls, erected for it by a Jewish gentleman of Bradford, Eng. It stands at the head of Tel-Abib's main street, and the school is the pride and center of the Jaffa, indeed of the Palestine Jewish, community. Together with the Bet Sefer la-Banot it attracts to Palestine hundreds who are debarred from an education by Russia's discriminatory legislation against the Jews. Russian Jewish mothers are said to form little societies, the members of which take turns at living in Jaffa and watching over all the children of their group.

The religious element in the New Settlement represented by the Mizrahi in the Zionist movement, while indorsing the modern pedagogical methods of the two schools, and agreeing particularly with their use of Hebrew as the exclusive language of instruction, was not satisfied with their attitude towards religion, negative at best they maintain, according to some critics actually irreligious. This dissatisfaction brought about the establishing of the Tahkemoni, on the pattern of the German Realschule. Only six years in existence, it has already over two hundred boy pupils, and it is contemplating a building worthy of Tel-Abib. For girls the Tahkemoni makes no provision.

In Jerusalem a similar division occurred between the partisans of different attitudes towards religious teaching. In the year 1909-1910, two schools with Hebrew as the language of instruction were opened, the Heder Torah for those who desired a school complying at once with their religious standards and with the generally accepted requirements of modern times, and the Hebrew Gymnasium, like that at Jaffa, for the element that takes the stand that the home not the school must determine the religious development of the child. The first has about seventy pupils, and is subventioned by the Hilfsverein, which has planned the curriculum; the second, supported with funds gathered largely in Galicia, has about one hundred and twenty-five pupils.

One of the most important educational projects yet conceived for Palestine is the Jewish Institute for Technical Education in Haifa. The Wissotzky family of Russia donated the first $100,000 towards such an institute; Mr. Jacob H. Schiff brought the project within the realm of the possible by a similar sum of $100,000; the Hilfsverein added a large gift from its Cohn-Oppenheim Foundation; the National Fund gave the land, to the value of $20,000, for the building as a perpetual leasehold; and larger and smaller subscriptions and scholarship funds were collected, particularly in America. The managing board was composed of representatives of all these various interests, and the leading officers were identical with those of the Hilfsverein. When the building was all but ready, in 1913, an unfortunate difference of opinion arose as to the language of instruction. The Zionists withdrew from the management, and when peace was restored, further complications, into which it is unnecessary to enter here, led, in

March, 1915, to the forced sale of the school building, which was bought in by the Hilfsverein for the sum of $56,250.

During the controversy feeling ran high in Palestine. The younger generation looked upon the conflict as of decisive importance. Their Hebrew mother tongue was contemned, they felt. Destruction menaced the world of resuscitated Hebrew ideals for which their pioneer fathers had struggled. The pedagogic objection, that a scientific nomenclature had not been sufficiently developed in Hebrew for it to serve as the medium of instruction in a technological school, was answered simply by pointing to the Jaffa Gymnasium. The opponents of the Hilfsverein plan in Palestine withdrew their children from all the schools of the German society, and established a parallel series of eight schools: a Teachers' Seminary and Commercial School, a boys' and a girls' school in Jerusalem, courses for Kindergarten teachers, together with Kindergartens, a night school in Jerusalem, a boys' school in Jaffa, and a boys' school in Haifa; and in some of the colonies self-taxation has replaced the Hilfsverein subsidy. The Zionist Organization has assumed the budget of nearly $31,000 for these schools, though such activity does not lie directly in its scope.

The deplorable results are patent: a duplication of effort and expenditure in a cause in which forces and funds are small enough; the loss of unity in effort in a country sufficiently distracted by division; and the delay in opening an institution from which Jew and Arab alike had expected great things. Harbors are waiting to be built; bridges and roads are needed; railroad expansion has hitherto depended wholly on imported brains and skill; irrigation plants must be multiplied; and

Jewish students denied by Russian autocracy their right to an education have lost a cherished hope.

The last word in the controversy, one cannot help but think, will not be spoken in Berlin, or in New York, or in Moscow, but in Jerusalem, and there not by this generation or by leaders, but rather by the processions of school children, on whose breath the world depends, as they wend their way singing to Moza on Hamishah Oser be-Shebat, the Palestinian children's Arbor Day, or when they frolic on Lag be-Omer on the heights encircling Jerusalem, or when, as members of the widespread Makkabi athletic societies, they respond to the calls made upon them on all public occasions.

The subject of the higher education has not yet been exhansted. At least passing reference must be made to the nine Yeshibot of Jerusalem, with their 800 students, institutions and students both supported at a cost of about $60,000 annually. These Yeshibot are partly Hebrew seminaries, partly Hebrew research institutions, the latter in the sense that the students are scholars that devote their life to the cultivation of Hebrew lore.

One of the most valuable undertakings, originated and fostered by the Odessa Committee, is the Teachers' Union, formed by the conference of teachers held in connection with the Kenessiah of 1903 in Zichron Jacob. The association has manifold objects, all tending to develop a unified standard of Hebrew education in Palestine, to which the schools will gradually conform and so constitute a completely graded system. When once the olive plantations of the National Fund are full-grown and yield a revenue, which according to its statutes is to be devoted to the completion of the system of education, the preliminary activities of the Teachers' Union will be recognized as fundamental.   It has drawn up curriculums for schools, and has stimulated the production of Hebrew text-books, which are issued by its publication society Kohelet.   Among its notable achievements are the founding of vacation courses for teachers and the holding of lectures and evening classes for adults.   It has stated conferences, and issues two magazines, Ha-Hinnuk, a pedagogic bi-monthly, and Ha-Moledet, for children, both, needless to say, in Hebrew. The language—developing it for pedagogic and daily uses, and awakening love for it among the people—is one of its main purposes, as it is the only purpose of the Waad ha-Lashon, the "Hebrew Academy," which is watching the coining of words and the growth of the language in the new literature and on the street.

Of the libraries in the villages mention has been made.   The central library of the whole country is at Jerusalem, Midrash Abrabanel it is called, founded by the B'nai B'rith lodge of Jerusalem, and enlarged in 1892, by the library of Joseph Chasanowitz of Bielistock, in honor of whom " Ginze Joseph " has been added to the name of the institution.   Every effort has been put forth to make it a central library for the whole Jewish world, by having Jewish authors deposit a copy of their works in it as they appear—a sort of supplemental copyright duty.   The object has not yet been attained.   It has only about 35,000 books, over half of them Hebrew.   The bibliographical treasures of Palestine are stored not in this library, but in the Yeshibot of Jerusalem, Hebron, Tiberias, and Safed, and in the private library of Mussayev, a Bokhara Jew, a devotee of the Cabala.   His library consists of rare printed books and manuscripts, and with them are exhibited his art treasures, for he is an art connoisseur besides being a student of the Zohar and a bibliophile.

In Jaffa is the Shaare Zion library with 6000 volumes, established by the Odessa Committee, which is the patron of libraries in Jerusalem, Haifa, and Tiberias besides. It is resorted to by the Jews of the colonies in the vicinity as well as by Jaffa Jews, and it is housed by the Jewish club. The Workingmen's Clubs in Jerusalem and Jaffa also have collections of books, and the Jerusalem Bet ha-Am has 4300. The last institution is the gathering-place for the young people, who are attracted to its newspaper and game room, and who go to it for their society meetings and their social gatherings. In all the urban centers there are mutual aid societies that have a semi-social character. Clubs are beginning to spring up, and the B'nai B'rith has lodges in Jerusalem, Jaffa, Haifa, Safed, and Zichron Jacob.

Other recent institutions are the two music schools, one at Jaffa and one at Jerusalem, the pupils of which occasionally give concerts. A collection of songs, many of them of recent Palestinian origin, has been issued, and as many of the schools have their athletic Makkabi brigades, so many of them have their school orchestras and glee clubs.

The press with only two exceptions is in Hebrew. The exceptions are a Spagniol paper, El Liberal, and one in Yiddish, Ha-Pardess. There are two dailies: Ha-Or and Ha-Herut; Ha-Moriah, in the interests of orthodox Judaism, appeared three times weekly (it ceased publication a short while ago); there is also a weekly, Ha-Ahdut, a workingmen's paper; the semi-monthly Ha-Poël ha-Zaïr, originally the organ of the Workmen's Union, but latterly representing the New Settlement in general; Ha-Meassef, a monthly; the children's monthly Ha-Moledet, and the bi-monthly Ha-Hinnuk, the pedagogic organ of the Teachers' Union; Ha-Meïr, a literary and scientific quarterly; Ha-Faklai, an agricultural periodical, the organ of the Union of the Judean Colonies; and Jerusalem, the useful annual issued by Abraham Moses Luncz, the scholar and devoted communal worker, who, himself blind, has been eyes to many afflicted like himself and by his researches a guide through Jewish Jerusalem and Jewish Palestine.

Of publication societies Kohelet has been mentioned. There are others: Yefet for literary productions, and Le-Am for popular scientific brochures, of which it has issued some seventy—all of which goes far toward explaining why there should be thirteen printers' establishments in Jerusalem alone.

Among the brochures issued by Le-Am is one on the diseases prevalent in Palestine. Two of the most widespread and common, malaria and trachoma, are both preventable and curable, provided they are not merely treated with a view to relieving individual patients, but are also investigated as to the fundamental causes, and measures are taken to remove the causes. In the open country the marshy stretches with their colonies of mosquitoes and in the cities the defective cisterns also offering a shelter to the insect pest, are sufficient to explain the malaria scourge.

The first effective step towards an intelligent campaign against malaria was taken in 1912 by the establishment of a Health Bureau in Jerusalem by Mr. Nathan Straus, equipped to meet many of the existing sanitary needs. The Turkish Government realized the value of the institution for the country at large. When, during the first Balkan War, there was an outbreak of cholera in Tiberias, the director of the Health

Bureau was requested to hasten thither, and his services in stamping out the epidemic in short order were recognized by the Government. Again, during the present war, the Government turned to the Health Bureau for scientific co-operation. All the analyses required in the Palestinian army hospitals have been made by it; it has had to furnish the typhus vaccine, and hold itself in readiness to combat epidemics as they made their appearance. At the same time its trachoma and malaria work for the civil population has proceeded, hampered though it, like all medical agencies, was by the shortage in medical supplies. Mr. Straus's Institute associated with itself the Society of Jewish Physicians and Scientists for Improving Sanitary Conditions in Palestine, and both co-operated with the German Society for Combating Malaria in Jerusalem. Up to the outbreak of the war the three agencies together constituted the International Health Institute. There are four departments of work in the Straus Bureau: the hygienic division, with a special branch for the treatment of diseases of the eye, a bacteriological and a serological division, and a hydrophobia division. Formerly the victims of rabies had to be hurried to Cairo or Constantinople. The Bureau has issued two reports, one on malaria in Jerusalem and one on the infectious eye diseases in Palestine.

Since the same year, 1912, there exists in Palestine also a Jewish Medical Society, which holds conferences at stated times, and issues its Transactions quarterly in Hebrew. These two medical agencies will doubtless succeed in making Palestine lovers pay serious attention to the sanitary needs of the country. It has long been known that a large percentage of Jerusalem's ills are due to the lack of an adequate water supply and the dependence on defective cisterns. Elsewhere in Palestine, in Jaffa and in the villages, the question of water is given the first place; in Jerusalem alone public opinion has not been aroused. It has moreover been demonstrated that it would require no great engineering ingenuity and not excessive means to draw water into Jerusalem from the springs and pools near-by. A year ago it was announced that the concession for this great improvement together with the lighting of the city and electric transportation facilities had been awarded by the Government to a French syndicate. The report was greeted with joy, for the undertaking would mean health and real prosperity for the Holy City, so beloved and yet so stricken.

A LAND OF POSSIBILITIES

Date of Forecast—Misconceptions—National Groups in Ottoman Empire—The Red Ticket—Fertility of Land—Methods of Cultivation—Mineral Products—Industrial Possibilities—Markets and Shipping Facilities—Imports and Exports—Rise in Land Prices—Railroad Expansion.

The foregoing presentation has insulated the new Jewish work in Palestine from its background and environment, as though it were wholly independent of and unconnected with them. It is hardly necessary to assert that the setting is of first importance. It amounts to a truism to say that however strenuous the efforts of the Jewish world to open up Palestine to home-hunting Israel, they will be unavailing in the end unless the desire and will of the Jewish people are endorsed by general conditions.

Before the possibilities of Palestine as a land of Jewish immigration are set forth, there must be clearness on one point. As the specific description of the New Jewish Palestine here given should be taken as dated a year ago, before the outbreak of the war, so the general statements now to be made will be based on what was then, not on what the fortunes of war will bring forth, or, without our cognizance, have already brought forth. This chapter purports to be not prophecy or political speculation, but a forecast on the basis of nature's and man's work in the Near East.

There are current phrases and statements that have created an atmosphere of haziness and misconception on the subject of Palestine. The catchword about the " immobility of the East " is re-inforced by the familiar Jewish expression, " going *back* to the land of the fathers." They impart a reactionary flavor to the immigration movement toward Palestine. The casual tourist has long been spreading reports about the sterility of the land, and misapprehensions prevail as to the character of Turkish rule.

To begin with the last: Reference has been made to the autonomy granted by the Ottoman system to national and religious groups. In the Orient the two terms are all but synonymous. By a sort of home-rule system freedom is enjoyed by all such groups to order their internal affairs as their traditions dictate. They administer them as independent bodies. In all that appertains to the complex fiscal administration they are of course held as strictly to account as are citizens and residents in other countries. With especial reference to the agrarian law, which, based in part on old feudal relations, is peculiarly involved; and likewise with reference to the system of imposts, which is to a very large extent a system of agricultural taxes, the Ottoman code, since the adoption of the Constitution in 1908, has been undergoing changes that are calculated to bring it into line with the requirements of a developing country.

In one respect Jews labor under a special disability. Admission to Turkey depends upon the presentation of a passport viséed by the Turkish consul of the traveler's home-land. Until five years ago the passport thus viséed had to be deposited at the port of entry, and for inland use a Turkish document was issued instead. This rule has been abolished for all but Jews coming to Palestine. Since 1888, on their arrival they are handed the "Red Ticket," good for only three months and marking them as Jews from foreign countries. This is in direct contradiction to Turkey's uniform treatment of her resident native or naturalized Jews, which places them on an absolute parity with her other nationalities. Though the regulation in respect to. the time limit is more honored in the breach than the observance, at intervals it has been enforced with punctilious severity. In any case, it is a stigma that should be removed. And it can be removed by the Jews of Palestine themselves as soon as they become naturalized Ottoman subjects in sufficiently large numbers to influence the course of events, not only in regard to this particular, but in the many ways for which the Constitution of 1908 has leveled the path. Hitherto Ottomanization has not appeared urgent, on account of the Capitulations and other means of obtaining the rights of extra-territoriality, under which Turkey granted a large measure of jurisdiction to foreign consuls. "Nationals" registered with their consuls, to whom they resorted in case of legal or political difficulties. Since the system of Capitulations has been abrogated, it is obvious that Ottoman citizenship has assumed a new dignity and a new importance for the Jew in Palestine. The way is open for him to become a civic force in village, town, province, and state.

So far as Palestine is concerned, the land cannot be held responsible for the prevailing poverty. The experts say that, barring size, it has the conditions and therefore the opportunities of California. Small as it is, it has varieties of climate and soil rivaling large areas elsewhere. Its surface is much diversified, from the alluvial plain at the sea-shore to the soft lava formation of the hill-country. The soils in various parts are adapted for all sorts of crops—for cereals, for truck farming, and for plantations. Some of the products have been mentioned incidentally. There are many others that might be enumerated: melons are abundant and delicious; figs, dates, and pomegranates thrive now and have a greater future; honey is produced in comparatively small quantities, but the yield can easily be increased; and tobacco has not been sufficiently studied in relation to Palestine. Wheat yields four and fivefold in the least propitious regions, eight to tenfold in Galilee, and fifty and sixtyfold in the Hauran beyond the Jordan. Vegetables are endless in variety and unexcelled in succulence.

Over against these advantages should be set the lack of copious watercourses in some parts of the country—but only in some parts. The environs of Hebron, for example, are rich in springs, and Transjordania in streams. At worst irrigation works must be resorted to; in many neighborhoods an intelligent study of conditions will probably discover a remedy in the application of the findings of modern science and practice. The American dry-farming system and American implements, it has already been demonstrated, will solve problems in some sections. Fertilizers, cattle-raising with the animal humus thus produced, and long-term rotation of certain crops, promise results, and so does the restoration of the ancient terracing of the hillsides, which may yet furnish indirect proof that even Arabic vines can be made to produce a marketable crop.

After a long period of coupled neglect and abuse, it is necessary to call help of every sort into requisition, especially in a country in which it is admitted that all conditions demand the intensive farming that latter-day theory makes almost coequal with the economic progress of humanity, and that raises farming to an occupation demanding trained intelligence in the same degree as it demands physical endurance.

Though Palestine is not rich in mineral products, the bowels of the earth await exploitation no less than its surface. Asphalt, bitumen, salt, phosphate, bromine and iodine salts, sulphur, and petroleum are to be found, if in small quantities, in particularly good quality.   The Standard Oil Company is said to be preparing to explore for oil in the Dead Sea region. Building materials exist, though not in sufficiently large amounts to offset the dearth of wood, pending the success of the reafforestation work already well under way.   There is coal, but so little that in discussing industrial expansion wise heads are planning for products that require low degrees of heat application, as, for instance, the cement building material made by means of high mechanical pressure.   Others are thinking of the possibility of harnessing the climate and developing sun-motors of intenser power than those known hitherto.   The large beds of lime and gypsum suggest exporting possibilities, and the earth is full of pottery material, which has been utilized hitherto only in primitive ways.   The presence of alkalis has led to the manufacture of soaps, which rank second in the list of exports, as the indigenous sumach and valonea account for the existence of tanneries now as of old.

For the development of industries there is sufficient raw material: The manufacture of oils from sesame, olives, oranges, and aromatic and medicinal plants is in its infancy; hardly any of the by-products have yet been considered. Besides cognacs from grapes, spirits from cereals suggest themselves, as well as non-alcoholic drinks from grapes. Wheat is already being used for maccaroni. The canning of fruits and vegetables and the preserving and conserving industries have not yet received serious consideration, in spite of the endless opportunities that exist and the admonition given by California's success. Silk culture was tried in Rosh Pinnah, and abandoned in 1906, but, if one notes the results achieved in the Lebanon district, as evidenced by the export records of Beirut, one cannot believe that the reasons will remain conclusive forever. Glass was once made at Tantura, Baron de Rothschild's factory near Athlit; that, too, with the sand of the dunes at hand, remains a fair hope in spite of the failure of the first attempt. Sugar production ought to be possible on a large scale in a land that can grow both beets and cane. With herds of fat-tailed sheep "upon a thousand hills," woolen products are not impossible along with the exporting of the raw material already done on a modest scale. Bezalel will develop carpet-weaving, and its copper and brass and silver products even now compete in exporting value with the mother-of-pearl articles of Bethlehem. There are a number of machine shops in Jaffa and Haifa. They will multiply with the plantations needing motors and irrigation works, demonstrating that there are openings for industries for which the raw materials must be imported, and such openings will increase with the modernizing of the Turkish system of imposts now under way.

A large part of this outlined development naturally depends upon the growth of the population, as the growth of the population depends in turn upon the industrial expansion. But even at the present stage, much could be disposed of if it were produced. Right at the door of Palestine lies Egypt, which, someone has said, has its mouth wide open constantly that its hungry, capacious maw may be filled. Its native population as well as its visitors want much more than they get, and with proper regulation Palestine could supply vegetables, dairy products, poultry, and fruit, if nothing else, as it already supplies wines in considerable quantity. If markets at a distance are considered, shipping facilities in a region so near the Suez Canal are adequate. They have been growing steadily: At the port of Jaffa, from 1903 to 1910, the increase has been from 425 steamers, with a tonnage of 803,000, to 707 with a tonnage of 1,115,000; and from 340 sailing vessels, with a tonnage of 12,000, to 756 with a tonnage of 24,000. Haifa has a similar encouraging record, and Gaza has within a few years attained importance as a barley shipping place. Such progress has been achieved, though not one of the ports on the Syrian coast has a harbor. What may be expected of the Near East when the Haifa Institute sends forth engineers and builders?

The trade balances complement the story told by the shipping. In September 1912, the American consul at Jerusalem reported that there had been an increase of 200% in the value of Palestine exports and imports since 1900, and of 100% since 1905. The Anglo-Palestine Bank's figures corroborate his statement at least for the port of Jaffa, through which passes, it is said, 40% of the Palestine trade. From the Jewish point of view, on account of the proximity of the large colonies of Judea, Jaffa is most important, but when all the railroad connections now contemplated are finished, Haifa may begin to dispute the supremacy of the southern port. The table of the Anglo-Palestine Bank is quoted by Nawratzki as follows:

Year	Value of Imports	Value of Exports
1903	$2,200,000	$1,620,000
1904	2,360,000	1,480,000
1905	2,300,000	1,840,000
1906	3,300,000	2,500,000
1907	4,040,000	2,420,000
1908	4,020,000	2,780,000
1909	4,860,000	2,800,000
1910	5,020,000	3,180,000
1911	5,820,000	3,840,000

The specific figures for exports given by the American consul for 1910, 1911, 1912, and 1913 deserve attention. In studying them, the reader should not fail to take into consideration that 1912 and 1913 were the years of the Balkan Wars:

Articles	1910	1911	1912	1913
Almonds	$3,908	$6,667	$27,739	$43,798
Animals, live	26,200	24,819	21,849	25,350
Barley	.....	.....	6,083	16,546
Beans	9,264	.....	1,723	1,897
Bones	5,594	7,154	2,725	2,788
Colocynth	16,733	31,754	35,039	11,636
Dari (millet)	55,106	57,911	98,547	46,231
Fodder	9,722	5,013	3,407	4,231
Fruits	179,726	204,393	121,662	165,461
Hides	79,945	83,460	36,012	51,244
Oil, olive, and sesame..	32,260	72,900	19,466	30,512
Oranges	1,136,794	1,058,464	1,380,139	1,449,757
Raisins	36,187	42,217	53,960	50,806
Sesame seed	179,659	476,917	146,774	152,321
Soap	762,538	702,236	868,500	973,300
Souvenirs, religious	58,889	93,193	107,063	101,223
Vegetables, lupines	64,935	64,140	51,682	61,123
Wines and spirits	293,963	277,641	337,735	294,569
Wool	35,465	32,849	22,289	13,029
All other articles	82,942	216,699	72,997	145,995
Totals	$3,069,830	$3,458,427	$3,415,391	$3,641,817

And here are the tables of imports for the same years:

Articles	1910	1911	1912	1913
Acids	$27,662	$21,899	$10,706	$17,860
Animals, live	107,597	197,580	175,194	184,927
Breadstuffs: flour	439,606	597,119	232,502	733,016
Cement	28,081	40,538	39,419	38,202
Chemicals & fertilizer..	......	......	71,440	51,497
Coal	24,197	57,084	70,000	98,994
Coffee	104,220	107,355	145,995	252,571
Drugs	42,841	43,799	......	......
Fancy goods	16,680	117,088	172,761	159,621
Fish, salt and dried....	23,609	29,783	46,718	47,691
Glassware and pottery..	83,907	67,158	61,318	64,481
Hides and leather	79,709	96,065	71,538	76,890
Iron and steel, manufactures of:				
Bedsteads, iron	......	15,573	8,662	15,816
Hardware	105,938	122,636	177,627	156,701
Iron bars, girders, etc.	82,435	112,903	97,330	117,730
Iron, other	114,642	138,208	72,997	92,463
Machinery	86,734	71,294	97,330	74,554
Motors	34,185	35,915	68,131	62,047
Oil:				
Illuminating	212,411	207,946	173,534	394,186
Linseed and machine.	41,133	38,737	48,665	53,531
Olive	116,355	154,463	154,995	237,485
Paint	32,019	30,367	29,199	48,665
Paper and stationery...	86,454	102,002	34,066	43,798
Potatoes	17,553	22,288	23,395	21,412
Provisions	92,857	105,360	145,995	161,567
Rice	253,385	296,175	226,000	308,682
Sacks, empty	48,597	59,663	64,238	65,834
Salt	7,792	24,965	39,419	35,282
Soda, caustic	50,783	67,644	58,398	61,804
Sugar	364,553	315,544	202,446	260,844
Textiles:				
Cotton goods	1,179,954	1,276,678	1,182,949	1,171,853
Other	61,181	69,104	72,365	72,997
Tiles and bricks	43,275	34,747	24,332	37,958
Tobacco and snuff	323,275	351,361	243,325	327,515
Wines and spirits	53,345	76,404	93,500	52,071
Wood, manufactures of:				
Furniture, etc.	65,185	35,525	48,665	47,789
Lumber	222,307	391,267	486,650	520,715
All other articles	188,561	161,130	316,323	218,992
Totals	$4,863,018	$5,693,367	$5,288,127	$6,388,041

The above figures represent the dealings of Palestine with Austria-Hungary, Belgium, Bulgaria, Denmark, Egypt, France, Germany, Italy, Netherlands, Roumania, Russia, Turkey, the British Isles and Colonies, and the United States.

In another way the progress of Palestine is recorded in the rise of land values: in Petah Tikwah land that cost from $2 to $5 a dunam (a little less than a quarter of an acre) at the beginning of Jewish colonization enterprises, now brings from $12 to $40. Twenty-two years ago a parcel of land in Rehobot was bought for $800, and left unimproved. Two-thirds of it was recently sold for $2400, and for the other third the owner had an offer of $1600. In Tel-Abib land values rose four and fivefold in three years.

That the whole world has confidence in the expansibility of the Near East is shown by the network of railroads that has covered the region since 1892, when the Jaffa-Jerusalem Road was opened to traffic. Three years later Beirut was connected with Damascus, and after another ten years, in 1905, a short line was run from Haifa to the interior, at Beisan. Since then the last has been extended to the southern end of the Sea of Tiberias and thence to a junction with the Hedjas Road, which when completed, as it has already been for a long stretch, will follow the old pilgrim route from Damascus all the way down to Mecca. The Hedjas Road in turn is an offshoot from the Anatolian-Bagdad system binding Constantinople to the distant Mesopotamian city and sooner or later to the Persian Gulf. From Haifa's first junction at Beisan, close to Merhawiah, a branch is being built to Nablus and Jerusalem, so completing the circuit to the southern port, Jaffa, and from Jaffa, it is expected, travelers and freight will soon be transported to Port Said and Cairo by land. So, not only will

Palestine have its hinterland, eventually with connections all the way to India, brought close to it, but with an arm flung out northwestward Jerusalem will touch the great Atlantic coast cities in Western Europe, and southwestward the Cape-to-Cairo Road will bring it into communication with the extreme point of the African Continent. Palestine lying at the junction of the three continents of the Eastern hemisphere gathers all these bands of civilization into its bosom, and becomes again the great highway, not as once for armies of destruction, but for the forces of prosperous peace.

CONCLUSION

PALESTINE AND THE UNITED STATES

An Eastern Land of Jewish Immigration—Organization of Jewry Outside—War Relief Measures—Organization of Palestine Jewry.

In Jewish vision Palestine has always lain thus at the heart of the inhabited world. Therefore, even in the face of a universal war's brutal menace to international safeguards, its central, coveted position arouses in the " lovers of Zion " not apprehension of disaster, but rather a sense of exultation as to future achievement. Its memories, tasks, and opportunities, equally noble, challenged Jewish ability, and the gauntlet was taken up. Jewish penetration comprehended the trend of circumstances in the Near East, and Jewish pluck has in large measure liberated the resources of Palestine.

The crisis evoked by the war has thrown the subject of the Jew in Palestine in sharp relief upon the canvas of Jewish life. In minds and hearts stirred by the suffering in strife-torn Europe, the question rises to the surface: Are the leaders of the Palestine movement prepared to assert that the Eastern land is ready for a mass immigration from comparatively near-by Russia, Roumania, and Galicia?

No categoric answer can be given. Palestine is not yet a land for immigrants in the same sense as the United States with its boundless spaces, its unlimited possibilities, its developed opportunities—with a place ready for every stalwart new-comer to slip into. Whether it will soon become a land of Eastern Jewish immigration as the United States is the land of Western Jewish immigration, will depend upon the attitude of the Jewish world towards the subject. Palestine Jewish immigration will long require the thoroughly organized and unified assistance of the well-established, non-migratory Jews everywhere. But if outside Jewry for a time, and during that time ungrudgingly, will make of itself the exchequer of Palestine Jewry, the future of a considerable part of the Jewish race will indubitably lie in the expanding East.

Is there evidence that this is coming to pass? Is Jewry tending to unify itself for practical operations in Palestine as it has for two thousand years been all but a unit in point of Holy Land sentiment? On these questions the world war has thrown light. The Halukkah has indeed been almost entirely cut off in the lands in which the sword was unsheathed. It was to have been expected: the Halukkah is the tribute of the poorest of the poor nearly everywhere. That faith and interest in the cause were not paralyzed even by the bloodiest of catastrophes, was proved by the more prosperous among the Palestine lovers. From the German trenches in France, from England and her colonies, and from the battle line in Russia and Austria, the pennies still flow into the coffers of the National Fund, if not so copiously as in good times, yet with unabated confidence in the practical worth of the land that typifies to the mind and heart of the Jew the principles for which his people has stood always, and has suffered often, during its long history.

But the most striking testimony to the newer appreciation of the claims as well as the value of Palestine as a land of refuge has been afforded by America. In the course of this article there has repeatedly been occasion to refer to America's effective participation in Palestinian development. From the eighteenth century down to yesterday, the Jewish immigrant, too frequently forced by business and industrial pressure to deny in practice the claims of Jewish tradition which in theory he may yet avow as legitimate and desirable, nevertheless did not " forget Jerusalem." If at times the age-long devotion was pushed out of earshot, its voice made itself heard to good purpose at crucial moments. Over and above the tribute levied, with the help of an imperious custom, by the Meshullah Karigal and his uncounted successors, America has enriched Palestinian life with contributions that rise beyond the level of the ordinary. From Judah Touro down to the Zionist plan for an Emma Lazarus Garden City for Yemenites, it has had a realizing sense of the housing needs of a growing population. The influence exercised more or less indirectly, through the Waad ha-Kelali, by the North American Relief Society for the Indigent Jews of Palestine and the New York Society for the Relief of the Poor in Palestine, became a conscious aim in the attempts to systematize the Palestine collections during the last five years made by the Waad ha-Merkazi of New York and the Palestine Committee of the National Conference of Jewish Charities in the United States, the latter called into being at the instance of the Central Conference of American Rabbis. The same period of five years has seen a constantly increasing interest in Palestinian undertakings of large educational and social scope—agricultural development (the Jewish Agricultural Experiment Station), sanitation (the Straus Health Bureau), higher education (the Jaffa Gymnasium and the Haifa Technical Institute), philanthropy (the District Nurses System), and economic progress (Ha-Ahuzah).

The last group of interests implies a recognition of the change wrought in Palestine by the Zionist attitude and Zionist activities: the emergence of the Holy Land from the field of charity that was suffused with a lovable sentiment, upon the field of economic opportunity fortified by the same sentiment. The same recognition, raised to a higher power, is conveyed by the action called forth by the war. Hardly was it realized, at the outbreak of hostilities, that Palestine was isolated from Europe, whence came nine-tenths of its support, than energetic steps looking to its relief were taken in the United States. Without a moment's delay, the American Jewish Committee heeded Ambassador Morgenthau's warning that a generation's work was menaced with extinction, and no sooner formed, the American Jewish Relief Committee followed its example, both bodies supplementing the efforts of the Zionist Organization. The activities of the last agency illustrate best of all how vividly the Jews of America realize the value of what has been fashioned by Jewish hands in Palestine, and what its preservation may mean in the rebuilding of the Jewish world, which, if an appraisement may be made before the smoke of battle has cleared away, is suffering a third destruction of its sanctuaries compared with which the two others as well as the 1492 exile from Spain and the 1882 pogroms in Russia are insignificant in extent. At the beginning of the war it was apprehended that the International Zionist Organization with

its seat in Berlin would be paralyzed. A provisional administration was spontaneously instituted in the United States.
When, later, it appeared that the regularly elected Executive
Committee had not been disrupted, the provisional body
assumed guardianship of Jewish Palestinian interests. That
the American Zionists instinctively felt confidence in American
sympathy with Palestine endeavors corroborates what has been
asserted about the appreciation of Palestinian values by
American Jewry. The results of its appeal are none the less
instructive. Not only did it collect an Emergency Fund to
replace the sums usually raised in Europe as well as in
America for the maintenance of the Palestinian schools and
the Zionist enterprises in the colonies and the cities, but its
office became the clearing house for all concerned about the
fate of Palestine. Figures tell the story: Through the instru-
mentality of the American Jewish Committee and the American Jewish Relief Committee, $75,000 were sent to Jaffa, to
the manager of the Palestine Office, the head of the disbursing
committee designated by the Ambassador. In addition there
passed through the hands of the Provisional Executive Committee for General Zionist Affairs, up to May 31, 1915, the
sum of $335,359.29, of which, in round numbers, $79,000
was disbursed for the normal Zionist activities in Palestine;
$61,000, an undesignated relief fund, was distributed among
institutions and associations in proportion to their scope and
needs; and $167,000 was transmitted to institutions and indi-
viduals named by the donors. Finally, the American Jewish
Relief Committee and the Zionist Executive together secured,
at a cost of $84,627.81, the food supplies which, by the courtesy
of the United States Government, were carried to the Holy

Land in the Collier Vulcan, and distributed among Jews, Moslems, and Christians.

Because it typifies at once the value attached to the new life in Palestine and the method of relief mainly resorted to, one more act of American initiative and generosity should be recorded: the raising of a considerable part of a loan of $120,000 to tide the Palestinian orange-growers over the disastrous year in which the whole crop of a million and a half boxes of fruit rotted under their trees. Without the loan not only a year's harvest, but the orange-groves themselves, the product of a quarter of a century's labor and care, would have perished.

A part of the other funds transmitted to Palestine was likewise applied to loans to planters, business men, and artisans, and for the execution of public works in which labor could be employed. Though America did not succeed in feeding all the hungry, it is a solace to know, as has been reported, that not a single Jewish workingman in the colonies has been without employment during the long period of stress. This may be due to some extent to the enlistment of the Arab workingmen in the Turkish army, but largely it is attributable to the moneys from America and their wise application.

A large part of the credit for what has been accomplished belongs to Ambassador Morgenthau and his personal representative in Palestine, who planned the distribution of the first $50,000 on the spot. Again, a large part of the success achieved is due to the intervention and help of the United States Government, without which it might have been found impossible to transmit to their destination the moneys collected and advanced. And mention should be made of the friendly spirit displayed by the Turkish Government, which granted facilities and privileges to the helpers from abroad.

There remains to be noted the capacity for organization displayed by the Palestinian forces in the acute crisis, betokening an advance in development beyond anything suspected by the casual observer. In Alexandria, in Jaffa, in Jerusalem, in Haifa, the organization abroad met a responsive organization, surprising in the Kolelim and in the flotsam and jetsam of the Jewries of the world only lately gathered into Palestine. Even before outside help came, the New Settlement had demonstrated its economic resources. The colonies had stores for themselves, and out of their superfluity could for a time sustain the cities. The Jewish bank had staved off a panic by devising a system of checks to be circulated among its depositors. In a word, there has been displayed the spirit of self-help that may fitly encourage the hope that the gifts and loans that are the pledge of the Jewish world's confidence in the New Palestine will rescue the plantations, fields, and homes created by a generation.

In that generation's hand-to-hand struggle with natural and economic forces, it has gained still other victories. A language has been all but achieved. The educational system needs only the last welding touch. In the spirit of the Mosaic law and the prophets' ideals, there have been initiated social forms of living pervaded by charity and based on justice and righteousness.

This record almost justifies the historical Jewish sentiment for the Holy Land cherished by the Jew of the Old Settlement and by the Jew of the New Settlement—almost, but not wholly. The spirit of each must yet pervade the other. A creative force already resides among the Jews who have settled in Palestine. The dry bones of gifts from all over the world have been clothed with the habiliments of life, and long-scattered mem-

bers have been joined together into an organism. Jerusalem
has begun to assume in a spiritual sense the aspect of a city
that is " builded compact together," and Palestine of a land
of a renewed social and religious promise, while universal
Israel in the Diaspora, through an organized common endeavor
for the Holy Land, is becoming a revitalized spiritual communion. But there remain dissonant notes that must still
be resolved into the harmony of independent thinking and
accordant conduct. A physical, merely passive coming-back
to the " land of the fathers " would have been an anti-climax
to twenty passionate, yearning centuries. No more can one
be satisfied with a Jewish Palestine that is a " land of the
children " and nothing more—of a future, however comfort-
able, unhallowed by the past. One Jew and another and still
another may escape to Palestine from galling oppression.
Many have already found life there free and happy. But
more values and more positive values must be created to justify
the strenuous exertions of Palestine lovers and Zionists. A
compact Jewish community, composed of members happy
through untrammeled Jewish self-expression, must reconsti-
tute a Palestine spiritually worthy of the unique place it has
occupied in the history of human thought. *Ex Oriente lux*
must again be a true-saying, that the sacrifices in Palestine
and outside of the land may have been worth while. It has
been reported that a religious leader of the Jaffa community
is busy studying the law and practice of the Yemenites, which
differ from Ashkenazic and Sefardic law and practice, in
order that, discovering the origin of the differences, he may
point out the just method of harmonization. Sefardim and
Ashkenazim, and the groups of Ashkenazim among themselves, will learn to seek similar adjustments, and all together

will develop a synthetic theory to suit the enlarging and diversified need. So the law will live again, and practice cease to be the hollow echo of a former condition. When spiritual Jewish problems are grappled with tolerantly but earnestly, without the excommunications of the past or the indifference of the present, then the Jew's whole personality will be brought into full play, and for the first time in two thousand years he will in one spot at least fashion all the manifestations of his life in a Jewish mould.

BIBLIOGRAPHICAL NOTE

What has been presented in outline in the above article, and for the most part without corroborating statistics, may be found in industrious detail in two recent publications, to which the present writer desires to express her deep indebtedness:

Palästina Handbuch, by Davis Triétsch. Jüdischer Verlag, Berlin, 1912 (3d ed.).

Die jüdische Kolonisation Palästinas, by Dr. Curt Nawratzki. Verlag Ernst Reinhardt, Munich, 1914.

The second book named falls short only of being the archives of the Jewish colonies in Palestine, so complete is the information it offers. An excellent feature is a full bibliography (PP. XI to XXI), to which may be added the following:

Zionist Pocket Reference, by Israel Cohen. Federation of American Zionists, 1914.

Zionist Work in Palestine, Ed. Israel Cohen. T. Fisher Unwin, London, 1911.

Zionistische Palästinaarbeit, by A. Böhm. Zionistisches Zentralbureau, Vienna, 1909.

Fünf Jahre der Arbeit in Palästina, by Dr. E. W. Tschlenoff. Jüdischer Verlag, Berlin, 1913.

Genossenschaftliche Kolonisation in Palästina, by Dr. Franz Oppenheimer. National Fund, Cologne, n. d.

Gemeineigentum und Privateigentum an Grund und Boden, by Dr. Franz Oppenheimer. National Fund, Cologne, n. d.

Merchavia. A Jewish Co-operative Settlement in Palestine, by Dr. Franz Oppenheimer. National Fund, New York, 1914.

Sefer ha-Zikkaron ha-Yerushalmi, by N. D. Freiman. Jerusalem, 5673.

Die ansteckenden Augenkrankheiten Palästinas und ihre Bekämpfung, by Dr. Arieh Feigenbaum. 1913.

Im Kampf um die hebräische Sprache. Zionistisches Central-bureau. Berlin, n. d.
Jewish Schools in Palestine, by Norman Bentwich. Federation of American Zionists, New York, 1912.
Report to American Jewish Committee, by Maurice Wertheim. Pp. 360-365 of the present issue of the AMERICAN JEWISH YEAR BOOK.

The map on p. 24 showing the Jewish villages, settlements, and estates in Palestine is a reproduction, with slight changes, of that drawn by Mr. Davis Trietsch.

The writer desires furthermore to acknowledge gratefully her obligation for data obtained from Mr. E. W. Lewin-Epstein, of New York, and Dr. S. Kaplan-Kaplansky, secretary to the National Fund.

CPSIA information can be obtained
at www.ICGtesting.com
Printed in the USA
BVOW06s0836150917

494987BV00012B/83/P

9 780282 010584